Dedication

For Dan, my husband, my rock

Table of contents

My Old Rocking Chair

My Old Rocking Chair

By, Lulu Gee

*Congratulations on winning
'Best of Show' 2019.*
Lulu Gee

Shoestring Book Publishing, Maine, USA

My Old Rocking Chair

Paperback

ISBN: 978-1-943974-23-8
Library Of Congress Control Number: 2018961683

Published by;
Shoestring Book Publishing.
Maine, USA

Layout and design by Shoestring Book Publishing

For information address;
shoestringpublishing4u@gmail.com
www.shoestringbookpublishing.com

vii

Preface

To sit and dream perchance to write a verse,
Seems wonderful from my old rocking chair,
And just a means to gently intersperse
A fairy-tale with castles in the air.
I close my eyes and slowly I coerce -
A fantasy where I'm the grand compere.
And with a few strokes from my poet's hand,
I'll spirit you away to wonder-land.

For legends need someone to tell the plot
And from my rocking chair I see it all,
From knights and Kings and tales of Camelot -
To dragons whence the battles they befall.
I fantasize of fables time forgot,
From mermaids, who with wizards can enthrall.
To unicorns and elves who understand –
My joy as I perceive their wondrous land.

As sunlight falls like stardust on the floor,
My rocking chair transports me ever high,
Where storks with new born babes fill me with awe
And witches in tall hats on brooms fly by.
'Tis here I write of myths amid folklore
To wish upon my dream tree in the sky,
Then board my sailing ship as I had planned
And in my dreams float to a magic land.

Acknowledgments

I would like to acknowledge my husband, Dan Lake who has never wavered in his belief of me.

Also Allpoetry.com for giving me the platform to learn my craft and the wonderful poets I met there who encouraged and gave me the confidence to write and present myself to the publishing world.

Introduction

Many years ago I was blessed with meeting a beautiful woman who I quickly fell in love with, Lulu Gee.

At the time we were both writing poetry, my poetry sometimes had political undertones and could be construed as being dour while Lulu's was bright and beautifully written.

She is an artiste that takes great care to work within the strict perimeters of her craft and anyone who understands what I am saying will tell you that to be able to write about Love and Passion, Faeries, Leprechauns, Seasons and Wildlife, all intermingled with grace and humour, tears and pain, within the tight confines she adheres to is a credit to her craft.

Her words will transport you to another place and time where everything is truly possible.

This book is but a fraction of her entire work and she is an inspiration to all rhyming poets that we both feel, are not always given the credibility they deserve.

I might add I married this beautiful poet and have never been happier in my entire life...

Dan Lake

Out and About ....

Seasonal Bliss

When my garden's bare of roses
On a cold mid-winter's day,
And the dormouse still supposes
Spring is very far away,
I can see the coolest lilac,
Greys and opals blushing pink,
Shades of winter playing havoc
'Til the spring peeps on the brink.

When my garden's less half shaded
On a day when seedlings swell,
And the blackbird's more than jaded
Singing clearer than a bell,
I can see the leaf-buds greener,
Moss to lime and lichen too,
Shades oft' seen in the marina
Tangled soft 'neath skies of blue.

When my garden's full of flowers
On a warm midsummer's day,
When I've lazed for hours on hours
Without anything to say,
I can see the colours clearly,
Purples, amethyst and rich
Shades of peacock shinin' steely
Silver-greens to help bewitch.

When my garden's feeling sleepy
On a cool, crisp autumn day
While the leaves are falling deeply
Blowing ev'ry known which way,
I can hear the grasses quiver,
Beating gently as a drum,
Where the orchids sadly wither
Warning earth winter has come.

This Morning ....

I strolled early this morning as spring was almost due
while snow fell softly silent
and mice play'd peek-a-boo,
with loveliness surrounding that for a while was mine -
I mused on nature's beauty,
beneath a cypress pine,
its boughs so heavy laden o'er ferns in dappled light,
no longer green and vibrant
but speckled, snow-flake white.

From icicles, a sparrow drank from a dry-stone wall,
disturbing creepy-crawlies,
appealing, moist and small
and canopies of hawthorns stretched 'cross the bridle path,
as robins, wrens and bullfinch
sought the magpie's wrath –
While squirrels high in branches were vexed and shied away,
a spider scuttled past me
with hopes of catching prey.

Two deer and then another peered through the mottled grove,
their coats the softest velvet
their eyes the deepest mauve,
insinuating shyness with beauty so divine,
beneath a sky of paleness,
of winter's own design -
A tapestry of splendour I so enjoyed today ....
With hopes to dream perchance tonight,
as snug and warm as they.

Past Winter ....

The morn's no longer misty, the night's no longer cold,
Now daffodils are dancing in gowns of saffron gold.
For winter's left my garden beyond the southern sun,
I know this, for the dormouse slow whispered, 'spring's begun.'

Here golden comes the sunlight with ne'er a sorrowed care
For anything not blooming, diaphanous and fair,
Nor cares a fig for flurries of snow in winter skies,
When linden leaves are falling past summer's sad demise.

The barefoot child's now playing while ladies on the green,
Sit idly reminiscing, here, there and in-between -
Iris and tulips blooming, where borrowed shadows sigh,
Past winter clouds grey, brooding in this my half of sky,

Whitstable Autumn ....

From the harbour wall I see
Out beyond the slip,
Far horizons wave to me
Where the breakers dip,
Cooler winds from northern skies
Blow this autumn day,
Like a monster, who can tell?
Drifting, cool and grey.

Clearer now against the sky,
High above the shore,
Sea-gulls swooping, loudly cry
O'er the breakers roar,
Louder than my thoughts today
Here now, safe and warm,
Framed in fleece on aging limbs
Flinching from the storm.

Before Winter

Earth surrenders harvest crops,
Fields of corn and strong limbed men -
Shoots and prospers, blooms and drops,
'tis the autumn, here again.
Apples, berries, baskets fill,
Apricots are turned to jam,
Trees and hedgerows over-spill,
Pumpkin chutney, roasted ham.
Morning dew and pearly mist,
There is much of earth to know -
Sweet of scent still warmly-kissed,
Winter beckons full of woe -

My Name Is ....

Sometimes I can be early, more oft' I'm rather late,
I don't have clocks to wake me
On any given date.
You'll never hear me coming, my footfall's fairy-light,
But every year I'm re-born
To ev'ryone's delight.
I herald in the tulips, snowdrops and iris too,
Sometimes an early primrose
Begowned in pink and blue.
I beg the trees to blossom and frozen brooks to flow,
And coax so many splendoured things
To flower row 'pon row.
I serenade the dormouse, still snoozin' 'neath the hay
Before I tease a climbing rose -
To share her fine bouquet.
I shade the groves and woodlands, to make the bluebells ring
And all the songbirds love me ....
They know my name is Spring.

Soon it shall be Spring

The north east wind is blowing still;
it's almost early spring,
when every poet finds his quill
and every bird his wing.
I long to kiss a sequined moon
to gently wish and slowly spoon.
  I long to kiss
  I long to kiss
and bathe where silver skies illume.

The north east wind is blowing still;
hoar frosts are all but gone,
while crocus dance upon the hill
no longer pale and wan.
I long to see springtime is here
to dream by waters crystal clear.
  I long to see
  I long to see
a love most tender, pure and dear.

The north east wind is blowing still,
as clouds unfold on high,
for this hour brings an icy chill
through veils of writhing sky.
I long to hear the young curlew
and pheasants in the tall bamboo.
  I long to hear
  I long to hear
my love betroth a love so true.

Spring

Will the Spring embrace my garden
With the joy of blooms to come,
Snowdrops in their bridal dresses,
Crocus and the bees low hum.
Hellebores and tulips nodding,
Petals turning to the sun,
Daffodils enhancing borders
Slow to greet me one by one.
Alliums in every colour,
Pom poms dancing in a line -
Interspersed with iris budding
Far below the old jade pine.
Primulas in shades of peacock
Full rejoice in warming rays,
'Neath a sky that dreams of Summer's
Ever-lasting, golden days.

October Storm

The winds blow strong, bitingly cold,
in skies that brood and cry today,
for while the leaves turn copp'ry gold,
the summer's warmth slow casts away.

With hope, the winds will cease to blow
the fragile spider webs now spun,
through apple trees where row 'pon row,
the harvesting has fast begun.

How silenced are the birds that sang,
by bugle blasts of stormy rage,
beside the cricket chants that rang,
as gales with rain take centre-stage.

For hours the rolling clouds sail by,
afar from yonder northern sea,
where ships beneath a rainstorm sky,
must steer their courses steadily.

Yet when the wind and rain has passed,
the calm shall touch my thankful breast,
when once again peace reigns at last,
for us to lay our heads to rest.

Summer Breeze ....

O summer breeze, please tell me
When autumn fills the air,
Where 'tis you like to wander
Leaving the trees so bare.

I heard tell from the dormouse,
She knows your secret well -
So here I'm left a wondrin'
Where'er you go to dwell.

And little robin redbreast
In worsted waistcoat bright,
Says, 'sorry' he can't tell me,
Why now you're out of sight.

There's no-one hears you going,
You're quiet as a mouse -
I looked for you all morning,
Disturbin' hens and grouse.

I asked the willow weeping,
Spider and badger too -
And agapanthus pondrin'
Her missing gown of blue.

O summer breeze, please tell me
Why you're no longer here,
When snow's looming in winter
Yet summer's nowhere near.

Beyond the Valley ....

Afar through yonder valley
Beyond the dappled glade,
I stumble 'pon a fairy
As daylight turns to shade,
And glow worms pearl and silver
Cast beams upon the grass,
While yet more fairy maidens
Dance gaily as they pass.

More oft' they'll beckon to me,
Then lead me by the hand,
To see the deer they're guarding
Throughout this mystic land,
Where colours shine a rainbow
Of pale to shades of shore,
As deer with coats of velvet
Kiss fairies they adore.

Each fairy wears a garland
Of daisies, pale as snow
And tiny leaves of juniper,
Found where the poppies grow
Below where willows weeping,
Take comfort from the sky -
Where all too soon they bid me,
'Farewell,' upon a sigh !

Castles In The Sand

Sometimes it's just the little things
That take your breath away,
A kiss from grandson after school
Before he runs to play
Along the beach of ivory
To waves that lick the shore,
As white as snow around his feet
Beseeching to explore.

The sea is turquoise, blue and green
With whispers to beguile,
As socks and shoes are cast aside
He beckons with a smile,
Beneath his feet the rippled sand
Feels velvet to his touch,
Anemones and crabs and shells
Don't bother him too much.

He sits content with sand castles
With turrets and a moat,
Defying every curling wave
That threatens it to float,
Yet while it stands it has a queen
And soldiers at the gate
And in his eyes a starfish waits,
About to infiltrate.

The sea is turquoise, blue and green,
A great pleasure to me
But now the waves are gaining strength
With timeless ecstasy,
Before my eyes the castles gone
With all the battles won,
So gather shells and shoes and socks
To take home, my Grandson.

Buttercup Meadow

Beyond the golden meadow
Where buttercups amass
Around between the clover
Where footsteps softly pass,
The heat of this midsummer
Makes every growing thing,
Seek spirit for survival
With glints of wondering.

The burden of the heat wave
May make the meadow cry,
As sun beats down with laughter
Causing the earth to dry.
Aroused, heaven will darken
For rain clouds to appear -
And skies, rumbling will tell us,
That thunder's all too near.

Yet rainfall soft as kisses
Will once again replete,
The hidden life that's stirring
So surely round our feet
And skies ablaze with splendour
Will make the shadows play
Beyond the golden meadow,
Upon this summers day.

Showers

Summer showers falling loud,
From a dull and hapless sky,
Bursting through each dancing cloud,
Pale, yet smiling, riding high.

Falling soft in arrow-flight,
Smoothly, dipping in-between,
All below 'neath heaven's light,
Shining lawns of em'rald green.

Glistnin' crystals drop and drip,
Leaping in warm summer's squall,
Over worms that slink and slip,
Shiny gemstones one and all.

Puddles ripple, whirl and list,
Shaking spiders in a spin -
Far from rendezvousing trysts,
Drenched like me down to the skin.

Beneath My Willow Tree

As I slowly close my book beneath my willow tree I look
at all the sumptuous coloured springtime gifts,
of daffodils in golden gowns, not for them poor hand me downs
and primroses amassed in fertile drifts.

The air feels warmer by the day as I watch a chaffinch play,
beneath this weeping willow where I rest,
and sparrows lovelier by far than they really think they are
are looking far beyond their very best.

My cat's still doing silly things over where my hammock swings,
trying to catch a kingfisher in flight.
'tis so heavenly to lie here watching bees and dragonfly,
amidst these wondrous things within my sight.

I hear the bells ring out for church, by the catkin'd covered birch
while blossoms burst their buds for butterflies.
Then when friends drop by for tea we sit beneath my willow tree,
and mallard chicks appear with hungry cries.

As I open up my book beneath my willow tree I look
to read a page on springtime poetry,
but digress with John McCrae and 'Flanders Fields' where poppies lay
and nature bows her head respectfully.

I Love To See the Narrow Boats

I love to see the narrow boats
Along the river Wey
And all the wildlife that I see
When walking every day
I take the dogs to sit awhile
Just by the old lock gate
And watch the crayfish being caught
By boys with smelly bait

I love to see the water vole
The otters and the mink
The swans with young so downy white
And adders that just slink
The cheeky little moorhen chicks
The mallard and the coot
But most of all the kingfisher
Clad in his turquoise suit

I love to meet the other folk
All busy having fun
The fishermen with patience sit
Until the day is done
And dog walkers I've known for years
With dogs I know by name
Of every breed, colour and size
Enjoying the same game

I love to see the boats that moor
And tether for the night
Then smell their dinner being cooked
With laughter at twilight
When badgers start to snuffle round
While owls are drifting by
And sometimes if it's very quiet
You'll hear a moonbeam sigh

My Summer Garden

'Tis neither fall nor winter-time,
my roses are aflame,
towards the western skies they lean
beyond the lilac frame,
where bamboo taller than myself
sways soft upon the breeze,
while spiders smarter than they look
spin high above the eaves.

I sit where fucshias over-hang
like dancers in disguise,
beside the honeysuckle scent
where beetles socialise
and magic drifts upon the air
as faeries in pale dress,
adorned with feathers fine as rain
enhance their loveliness.

Such humming from the honeybees
beyond the garden's fringe,
awaken lilies by the stream
where smiling ferns impinge,
while bluebirds in the topaz sky
sing soft their own sweet song,
I'll wonder at these pleasant things
for all the summer long.

I Wish ...

I often wish that I could sail
To far off lands beyond the pale,
Instead of sitting here depressed,
No longer looking at my best.
I'd sail the oceans far and wide,
With moonbeams shining as my guide,
Transporting me to desert isles,
With no computers or mobiles.

I often wish that I could fly,
Just pack my bags and say goodbye,
Instead of listnin' to the news
And Parliament's outrageous views.
I'd pilot my own private jet,
To fly to France for crepe suzette,
And there I'd sip Dom Perignon
Wearing the latest from Dior.

I often wish that I could ski,
To simply wave my hand and flee,
Instead of sitting in the cold,
With global warming taking hold.
If I could ski down a black run,
I think I'd done the pools and won,
Such an exhilarating fear -
To ski a mountainside that's sheer.

I often wish that I could sing,
To swing the blues and sing like Bing,
Instead of miming to a tune,
When all I want to do is croon.
If I could sing then I would dance,
In fishnet tights I'd kick and prance,
and live a life so avant garde,
In Paris as a communard.

I used to wish that I were dead
And free from mortal fear and dread,
To free myself from stress and strains,
But then I don't have many brains.
For now I'm happy as a lamb,
'Frankly my dear, don't give a damn,'
As long as I can come online
To make my verses flow with rhyme!

A Retourne to Autumn

How sombre now are mornings with skies of pearl so cold,
as trees let fall their showers of reds and molten gold,
but over where my heart lies the harvest is complete,
he's looking to the sunset at fields of garnered wheat.

As trees let fall their showers of reds and molten gold,
beneath the wind now stirring lies something to behold,
before blue skies turn mournful above the quiet hills
and busy hands grow weary before the winter chills.

But over where my heart lies the harvest is complete,
where in fields of goldenness the earth smells apple-sweet,
yet when the day grows cooler beneath a lazy sky,
wood smoke curls reflectively where sheep and cattle lie.

He's looking to the sunset at fields of garnered wheat,
where blackbirds have departed with appetites replete,
while gazing at his acres of which he'll never tire,
oh, if only I were there to quell my own desire.

Pretty Maids Of Summer

When days are lost in dreaming
beneath the golden sun,
in Summer each maid hurries
to curtsey one by one.

Iris with eyes dark fringing,
mid Rosemary's bouquet
can't rival Poppy's glory,
or Daisy's chain display.

And without question Lily
smiles, beckoning me near
to kiss her own sweet petals
in bloom again this year.

Alas, Bluebell's now fading,
'long with the blue of tide,
yet still Viola's peeping
more nervous than a bride.

While Cherry sheds her blossom,
Clematis, Jasmine, Rose,
begown themselves in colours
to strike a pageant pose.

Each have their own sweet beauty
with tenderness, among
the warming rays of summer,
immortally so young.

August Haze

'Tis summer in the meadow
where swallows trail a stem,
there in-between the clover
I follow after them,
where earth warms bare and stifling
from heat haze o'er the plains,
as warming rays of sunshine
so tremble for the rains.

And with each breath of summer
such memories unfold,
as spendthrift rays of sunshine
bear down, airless and gold,
yet southern skies will darken,
for rain clouds to appear
as thunder, rolling warns of
the storm now all too near.

When rainfall soft as kisses
will lovingly replete,
the hidden life now stirring
so surely round our feet,
and when again the skies clear
to pansy-blue from grey,
I'll praise the colours spilling
upon this summer's day.

Raindrops ...

Rain falls softly with a chill,
Laughing at me from on high,
Racing, calling me at will
From the storm now riding by.

Tulips by my window pane
Hold their pretty petals up,
Hoping for a drop of rain
In each tiny scarlet cup.

Voices whisper in my ear
From the pond beneath the trees,
Chanting, ever plain and clear
Through the rain, falling with ease.

Frogs and toads in chorus sing,
In the cool and dampened gloom,
Bathing as the rain's pouring
'Pon the lily pads in bloom.

O'er the sparkling stretch of lawn,
Pure as diamonds in the light,
Swift, my garden is reborn,
With the rain it glistens bright.

Spiders tremble by the stream,
Waiting for the rain to cease,
Tabby cats prefer to dream
Warm by fires on beds of fleece.

Earth worms slink and ripple soft,
In this rain-soaked heav'nly space,
As I hold my head aloft ....
Raindrops fall to kiss my face.

Today

Today I've seen such lovely things
I never knew could be;
Sunlight golden upon a jar
Of honey from a bee.

A snowstorm and a goose in flight,
High o'er the Lammas land
While children tumble out of school,
With books to understand.

A gift of flowers in a vase
With just a single rose,
Tight curled between the daffodils
Beneath a pretty nose.

Bed linen crisp as falling snow
With pillows plumped for rest.
A sweater bought just yesterday,
For me to look my best.

A poem penned to make me smile,
Or wonder 'pon a sigh,
Then walking with the dogs today,
Smiles from a passer-by.

An avocado green and ripe
To make my taste buds flow,
The crossword in The Telegraph,
A button I must sew.

And all because my love kissed me.

Such A Day ...

On a day when sunlight's shining
And the river's bathed in mist,
Far below a thousand hilltops
Where the spring and summer kissed,
Such a day aches for recalling
When upon my shadowed lawn,
Came a family of deer
Seeking food before the dawn.

There in early morning shadows,
While the mice were yet asleep
And the moon and stars were drifting,
Far beyond horizons deep,
I could see the willows tremble
As a fawn, scraped gently there
And the mother, eating roses
Sniffed the cold, forbidding air.

When the tallest trees are swaying,
On a gentle summer breeze
And the smallest boats are sailing
On the river and the seas -
I recall these gentle creatures,
Velvet brown and speckled white,
Shy and tentative, exploring -
Misty-eyed and shining bright.

The Journey ....

I was born deep in the valley,
I creep through grav'lly glens,
I stumble over rocks and stone
And saunter 'cross the fens -
I navigate along the way,
I race, I surge, I list,
I value nature's honesty,
Beyond the barren mist.

I roll 'neath alpine mountaintops,
I smell the snowdrops there,
I trust the landmarks guiding me,
Between the trees now bare -
I greet sand martins overhead,
I stoop 'neath bridges too,
I meet the rain and thunderstorm
While coots play peek-a-boo.

I grow beyond the valley now,
I swell with super force,
I leave the glens and rocks and stone,
And snowdrops mid the gorse -
'Tis now I hear the combers call,
With open arms for me,
Beneath a sky kissing the moon,
Toward the open sea!

Reborn ....

All is changing,(I can tell), skies illume with shine,
o'er the pasture, through the dell,
flawlessly divine,
like a vision to inspire poets sweet refrain,
prized by mortals own desire,
spring appears again.

Now below my window-sill, tulips white as snow
'neath the willows, tall and still,
blossom row 'pon row,
curving like a crescent moon here before my eyes,
on this lovely afternoon -
winter's in disguise.

Far beyond,(now I can see) past my garden wall,
all of nature's tapestry,
warm as Mother's shawl,
sapphire blue against the sky, green against the earth -
all l of this I can't deny,
spring has given birth!

Ready for Autumn

Almost a half a year's been spent
  I really can't say where it went,
But now the flowers have lost their frills
  And night falls early, cool with chills.

My roses blush softer than silk,
  Their petals creased, fade pale as milk,
Now shaking gowns of summer bloom,
  With ling'ring scents of sweet perfume.

While shadows soft, caress the trees
  To murmur sighs upon each breeze,
Their leaves of gold unfold from limbs
  Beneath a sky that shades and dims.

Fruit ripe and kissed in warm lit sun
  Slow whispers harvest has begun,
And so as earth puts forth her yield,
  Young, handsome men garner each field,

Yet now more distant is the sight
  Of moonbeams in the cool of night,
For in the summer they'd drift high
  To shimmer from a star-filled sky.

So now I'll rest my eyes and wait
For winter .... to unlock her gate.

No Longer Summer ....

No longer summer's here with me,
for now the skies are leaden grey,
o'er faded earth for all to see -
my bare and withered willow tree
this pale, aloof October day.

No longer does the blackbird sing
and troubles me to reason why,
before the snows of winter bring -
what some might think a paltry thing,
with shivers cold upon a sigh.

No longer do I see the blush,
below my aging weather vane,
of daisies in their second flush -
or eavesdropping to songs of thrush,
while walking down a country lane.
No longer is it summer ....

Mr. Snow And Robin

There's a snowman in my garden
With an enigmatic smile,
Wearing gloves to keep his hands warm
In a pattern called Fair Isle
And he's dancing in the snowstorm,
Twirling this way and then that,
Showing off his new red muffler
'Neath his balaclava hat.

And a robin in a waistcoat,
Ruby red in finest tweed,
With a pocket made precisely
For her over-flow of seed,

Sits upon a branch of willow
Singing slightly out of tune,
To the snowman dancing wildly
On this cold, white afternoon.

September Skies

Down where the dormouse gently sleeps,
Beneath decaying garden mould,
The ivy on the rowan creeps
As leaves in autumn turn to gold.
Bare is the earth and sharp of scent
For half the beauty of the day,
As birds eat berries with content
While squirrels secrete nuts away.

And while the rose shakes off her gown
Of lipstick pink and ivory,
My poppies all a tremble frown
As spiders spin in shrubbery.
Yet as the afternoon grows dim,
Clouds turn from grey to paper-white,
While sycamores groan limb by limb,
And beetles scuttle, taking fright.

The wind's loud blowing round the house,
While storm flies at my window pry,
But all is quiet as a mouse,
Inside where all is warm and dry.
The twilight hour is still and sweet
And like the cats I'm snug as they,
Denying winters mournful beat,
With thoughts of summer castaway.

The Curfew

The curfew now has sounded,
for dragonflies and bees,
while flames of autumn's season
burn amber-gold the leaves.

The far sky's warm and sparkling,
yet here beneath my sky
sit sloes on polished blackthorn
as veils of rain sweep by.

This is the gentle season,
where memories bring smiles
of summer days on beaches,
with golden sand for miles,
where children danced in sunlight
midst countless mysteries,
from rock pools, shells and starfish
and sea-anemones.

But now the days are shorter
with berries hanging still,
and spiders peer to welcome
another seasons chill.

The summer's deep in slumber,
with all her beauty seen -
'tis now the time for autumn
to wear the crown of queen.

Herne Bay Autumn

The days are getting shorter,
The nights are long asleep,
The fields of harvest re-sown,
The furrows wide and deep,
The lily-buds now blanch to milk,
The willows softly weep,
With sadness for the golden leaves,
They try so hard to keep.

The days are getting shorter,
The nights are cool and dim,
The lamps are lit in London,
The mist hangs on a whim,
The trees are kind, they understand,
The skylarks dart and skim,
O'er golden sheaves 'neath southern skies
And wood-smoke curling slim.

The days are getting shorter,
The nights seek out the light,
The linden leaves are falling,
The clouds bow pearl and white,
The ladies shiver in the park,
The harvest moon's in sight,
Above the tangled orchard smells
This stainless Autumn night.

October Days ....

From skies paler than charcoal,
Drift clouds pleading to burst
With rain to pour and cascade,
Appeasing nature's thirst,
To welcome this October morn,
Where Rose, with petals bowed -
Is strugglin' parched and wearisome,
No longer budding-proud.

With Maples changing colour,
From red to pink and gold,
I see the shiv'rin' spiders
Take refuge from the cold,
While winds blow like a trumpet's blast,
With echoes through the trees -
Now unadorned and bare of dress,
These cold October eves.

The Daisies and Dianthus,
Along with Coral Bells -
Now bick'rin' with Violet
Start saying their farewells.
To summer when the earth was kind,
Convivial and warm,
Where all my garden was a stage,
With wonders to perform!

Would You Believe

Would you believe a shower of rain
could make you wonder yet again,
how every drop trickles at will
to sometimes shock and sometimes thrill,
when pouring with a cool refrain.
Although each leaf, with marbled vein
bathes in the water,crystal plain
we curse but yet we need it still.
   Would you believe?
More distant than my window pane,
across the rain-kissed shady lane,
all colour floods my soul until
each birdsong voice is gently still,
no matter how my old ears strain.
   Would you believe?

Beyond the rain in afterglow
my flowers unfurl and bees follow,
upon the sun-kissed, gentle breeze
where swallows gather in the trees
to see the farmer plough and sow.
Yet as my spirits lift, it's though
strange blossoms tremble row on row
to melt my heart and gently tease.
   Beyond the rain.
A rainbow waits, tranquil, I know
where only loveliness can grow,
as all the colours beg to please
while steadily the grey clouds ease,
to skim the earth spinning below.
   Beyond the rain.

Cumbria

Oh! My heart's in Cumbria,
That for so long I've missed,
The blue grey hills and valleys
Of early Autumn's kissed.
For not since young I've seen it
Beneath a northern sky,
When at dawn in soft grey mist
I watched the clouds race by.

The lakes 'neath mountain summits
Are deepest peacock green,
With trees aflame in Autumn,
The like you've never seen!
For colours rich in texture
Are painting gold the hills
While heathers bathe in purples,
Ahead of winter chills.

All through this golden silence
By silver tarns aflow,
The low-land sheep are grazing
Where tangled breezes blow
And o'er beyond in Keswick,
You'll see the ospreys there,
Among the blue of shadows
Where sights of them are rare.

Yet should you walk on higher
To climb the tallest peak,
There's snow as white as crystal
Where clouds will brush your cheek.
My heart so loves this landscape
That Autumn's long desired,
The lakes and fells and mountains,
Where poets are inspired.

The bronze and gold this season
Will nestle on the brink,
Of shores beside pearl waters,
Where trout and salmon slink.
Oh! My heart's in Cumbria,
That for so long I've missed
But hope prevails I may return
To keep an Autumn tryst.

Thankful ....(Quatrain)

I feel my heart's an alpine spring,
As cool as crystal, sparking cold
And should I ask for anything
From hollows deep to caverns old.

Beyond this hour I'm worse than fool,
As shining clouds unfold on high,
Grey, tinged pink, slow drifting cool
Like blossoms, swaying on a sigh.

With petals perfumed lifting up
Their beauty to my half of world,
Resplendent to each 'spectant cup,
With blooms of ev'ry shade unfurled.

From palest rose to pigeon blues,
Such loveliness on ev'ry stem -
Awakening my poet's muse,
My spirit should evolve like them

How could I ask for anything,
When all I have this perfect hour,
I feel my heart's an alpine spring,
My essence, a resplendent flower.

My Autumn Garden

Now that my garden's close to sleep
There's not so much I must upkeep,
Although some leaves are hanging still
As twilight brings a frosty chill.

The beauty of the summer's gone,
Only the rose will linger on
As flower beds no longer cheer,
So pinks and reds shall disappear.

The oriental poppy bows
As though these are her final vows,
I haven't seen a snail in weeks
A clustering in slimy cliques.

Last week the hostas bade, 'farewell',
Surrounded by discarded shell,
While snails have feasted at a pace
So intricate, like antique lace.

And peonies, with heads aloft
Now stand fatigued and brownly soft,
As breezes tremble trees so bare,
Like spinning windmills in the air.

And round my door great spiders creep
Mid silken webs they spy and peep,
When cold enough they'll come indoors -
For Puss to torment with her claws.

Pale russets on the orchard floor,
A feast for badger's winter store,
Along with carrots and courgette
For when he ventures from his sett.

While Mister Mouse has locked his door
To sleep tight curled on leaves and straw
Yet squirrels still come down to see
Small tit-bits I've put out for tea.

And sat upon a golden bough,
A blackbird tries to tell me how
His birdsong must now surely cease,
Unlike the chatter from the geese.

Soon veils of rain will sweep the sky
And thunderstorms will surely cry
So I shall put away my spade
Until I hear spring's serenade.

Winter ....

As autumn's lease surrenders, no further fees to pay -
With wind and snow I'll travel upon my yearly way,
I'll cover grassy meadows and sprinkle ev'ry dale,
With veils of winter's colours to shimmer shades of pale.

I'll freeze the streams still flowing and wake Jack Frost from sleep,
To sharpen up his mem'ry with promises to keep -
All winter storms and blizzards hostile beneath your feet,
With flakes of snow soft driven and icicles from sleet.

I'll wake the moon too early, he'll sigh, but realise
You'll need his shine by twilight, across dark velvet skies
And all the lights in London will glimmer in the snow,
While late commuters dither as cold winds start to blow.

My rage will last 'til blackbirds and song thrush start to sing,
As winter's lease surrenders for rebirth into spring.

The Crystal Globe

Christmas in a crystal globe:
Santa is expected,
From a land beyond the sun
Over moonbeams one by one,
Coloured like his crimson robe:
With his gifts collected.

Toss the crystal ball aloft,
Flakes of snow surprising,
Paler than the morning light
Ankle-deep and shaken white,
Like a new-born, velvet soft
Ever mesmerising.

Trees a sparkle whisper low:
Santa is expected,
When the babes are fast asleep
On this night when slumber's deep,
Silently in candle-glow,
Christmas is reflected.

November Mourning ...

I love the shade of Autumn,
November time again -
when grey clouds roll to gather
before the steady rain,
'cross fields and mountain ranges
where cattle silent graze,
where Autumn's cloak surrounds them
slow falling to amaze.

Yet cool November's mourning
the heat of summer soil,
the ordered roses blooming
'tween honeysuckles coil,
amid the veils of greenness
beyond the shaded lanes,
beyond the woods and orchard
when warmth ran through my veins.

I love the mist filled distance,
brown leaves 'neath saddened skies,
the withered limbs of willows
with gath'ring mournful cries,
now days are lost in dreaming
before the winter snow,
before December's promise
of Christmas trees aglow!

Rime Mountain

The snow clouds swirl around my head for all the world is ice;
oh if only you were here, this could be paradise.
Beside the mountainside it's still and quiet as the grave,
with only tears from icicles in this my barren cave.

The snow clouds swirl like veils of gauze upon this cheerless day;
each marbled pink as raspberries, soft as an iced parfait.
what's surely happened in my heart, I cannot find the words -
not even to the mountain sheep or dawn awakened birds.

The snow clouds swirl in splendour as I smell the edelweiss,
picked tenderly just yesterday, the mountain's sacrifice.
I feel the spell is lifting that has made my blood run cold;
the magic castle's now in view, a talisman in gold.

The snow clouds swirl and slumber as I scale the icy piste;
the castle swings open its doors bestowing me a feast.
At last the tide is turning for true love will take its course,
as sure as moonbeams shimmering upon the winter gorse.

The snow clouds swirl but now I feel the kissing of the sun -
and hark, a thousand songbirds all in chorus, every one.
No longer do I see the cave below the clouds that swirl;
now all I see are twinkling stars of silver, gold and pearl.

Winter's colours

Winter is a sombre time,
Sombre, leafless season,
Sparrows seek out warmer days,
They have ev'ry reason.

Flying with a measured calm,
Tossed in skies together,
Softly brown, through veils of rain,
Coloured like the weather.

Once the autumn bids farewell,
Swift there comes a stir
From winter's faerie, frosty-pink
Begowned in velvet fur.
O'er the hedges crystal-white
Beneath a stooping sky,
Gentler than a thistledown -
On thermals flying high.

Winter is a sombre time,
Sombre, leafless season,
Reindeers roam on quiet feet,
They have ev'ry reason.

Lovelier than clouds of pearl,
Tossed in skies together,
Softly white as crystal snow,
Coloured like the weather.

Snowflakes

Snowflakes on a pretty nose,
Must be winter I suppose,
Soft they kiss the altered trees
Bare of summers verdant leaves.

High upon each gracious bough,
Clear and crisp all shining now,
Through the cold enchanting light,
Polished to a sparkling white.

For the snow shows whiter far
Here than earthly snowflakes are,
From some crystal globe-like scene,
Falling o'er the faerie queen.

All I see Jack Frost has made,
Pools of crystal, shores of shade,
'Til familiar landmarks seem
Vague, remote as last night's dream.

The Lonely Snowdrop

I saw a snowdrop yesterday
beneath a sky of pink and grey,
where nothing so far is in bloom,
where all is barren as the tomb.

No daffodil or crocus yet,
to herald Spring's own silhouette,
no tulip or forget me not,
nor hyacinth in china pot.

Anemones are still asleep
While primroses have yet to peep
And hellebores beyond the gorse
Will slumber 'til the Spring, of course!

It seems the earth's a silver lake,
with just this snowdrop wide awake
begowned in whiter shades of pale,
she stands alone, forlorn and frail.

December Dawn

At the dawning of the day
On the road to who cares where,
Skies roll pink and pearl and grey
Over blossoms swaying bare,
There's a newness to the morn
Shining brighter than a pin,
As the night turns into dawn
Showing spiders in a spin.

Hoar frost sparkles, crystal-white
On the road to who cares where,
Robins preen themselves in spite -
Of the magpies sitting there!
Boughs bend low with heavy dew,
Moist and chilled beneath my feet,
Ever beautiful, the view -
Fresh and clear and crisp and sweet.

Starlings swoop to meet the day
On the road to who cares where,
Teasing tabby cats at play,
Mildly showing some despair,
'Neath the sunlit winter sky
As the fox comes home to ground
To his family, while 1
Tell of wonders that 1 found ....

With Feeling ....

I Wish I Were A Poetess

I wish I were a poetess,
To write of lazy summer days
With picnics on a yellow beach
While watching quiet, lapping waves.
And maidens who, freckled by sun
Are sweet as pie and cherry-lipped,
Who stroll with lovers hand in hand
Beneath moonbeams silvery tipped.

And when the autumn shadows come
To blow away the leaves so green,
I'll write of clouds soft in the skies
O'er veils of rain on Halloween.
Or waking to a dew-lapped morn
Where gardens wish to sleep not stir,
Except for spiders spinning webs,
Except for mice with velvet fur.

My muse in winter's frost may sleep,
As will the hedgehogs under mould
Curl up and dream of seeds to eat,
'Neath warmer skies sprinkled with gold.
But I am greedy for a kiss
From stars that shimmer in the night,
Upon a land that's cold with snow,
Upon a land that's crisp and white.

In spring I'll see the fairies wake
To skim the air on dragonflies,
Bejewelled in greens and mystic blues
To halt my pen with blissful sighs.
I'll write of primroses in bloom
Begowned in every shade of dress,
Then close my eyes perchance to dream ...
I wish I were a poetess.

The Bride

She smiles behind a veil of cloud,
with bridal crown of pearl and gold
and through it green and dusky eyes,
betray her thoughts that now unfold.
Her wedding gown of tulle and lace
lay cast aside without a care,
a crumpled mass that lies beneath
her body, unadorned and bare.

Her voice is honey, dripping, slow
to whisper softly in the hush,
with drooping lashes purple-hued
upon her cheeks tinged with a blush.
She's like a blossom in a dream,
an orchid in the morning mist
awaiting warmth to gently stir,
her petals parted for a kiss.

Only the moon is dancing still
to bathe her body in his light
where sequins sparkle on her skin,
across the beauty of the night.
Now slow she bares her stockinged feet,
then with a touch upon her brow
she knows as sure as there's a sky,
she'll look no lovelier than now.

Rendezvous

As snowdrops bathe in sun with grace,
at our appointed meeting place,
then in the garden I shall peep
to wake the dormouse from his sleep,
when hedgerows start to need a trim ...
I have a rendezvous with him.

I hope that he will smile at me,
and if he does I guarantee -
my eyes will fill up to the brim,
because I've rendezvoused with him ...
I'll be enmeshed within his spell,
as if I'm on a caravel,
sailing exotic seven seas
to far-off lands and colonies.

He'll take my hand and kiss my lips
and fill my head with funny quips,
then I will nod and then I'll tease,
and give his hand in mine a squeeze,
We will declare our love's still true ...
thank God we kept this rendezvous.

Year Of Dreams

When the moon is riding higher
far above the twilight sky,
all the dreams that we desire
will in spring come flying by,
with a secret for the primrose,
with a secret for the trees,
with a secret for the bamboo
now tall, clicking in the breeze.

When the moon with maids are dancing
over city lamps that show,
all our dreams surely advancing
will in summer start to grow,
With a seedling from a poppy,
With a seedling from a pine,
With a seedling from the woodland
where I held your hand in mine.

When the moon's a silver bubble
in the early hours at dawn,
all our dreams with ne'er a trouble
will in autumn gather corn,
with a harvest full of sunshine,
with a harvest full of wheat,
with a harvest full of blackbirds
kissing rainbows round our feet.

When the moon is in the far sky
as the sun begins to rise,
all our dreams I dared to not die
will in winter realize,
with a banner streaming loudly,
with a banner now unfurled
with a banner that's been sleeping
for the most part of our world.

I Stole A Kiss

I stole a kiss –
A secret kiss
One starry night in June
When love rang out a melody
So sweetly sung in tune.
'Neath skies of darkest amethyst – I blushed – I turned away –
With thoughts of cupid's arrows,
With thoughts what Pa would say!!!

A Thousand Voices

Pray what has happened to my heart this cold November day,
I have a thousand voices in my head – what do they say?
They whisper like a summer breeze in skies of pigeon-blue,
But tell me naught that I don't know – they say that I love you.

The clouds of grey don't bother me for everything's in bloom,
Even the rose now withering, emits her sweet perfume,
You brought me daffodils today, reminding me of spring
And warmth that I hope soon will come with sun's ensaffroning.

I feel like I am born again, whatever can it be?
The road has been a lonely one but love has come to me,
At last a thousand voices are now chorusing in tune,
As I arrange the daffodils you bought this afternoon.

Am I The woman

Am I the woman ...
To keep your heart racing
When northern skies quiver
With cold air that's bracing.
When witches on broomsticks
In darkness are chasing
The warlocks asunder
Their terrors emplacing.

Am I the woman ...
Who when you are sleeping
Shall hold you close to me
To stop you from weeping.
When demons upon you
Are restless and leaping
And all through the night time
The spirits are creeping.

Am I the woman ...
To wake in the morning
With kisses of passion
As daylight is dawning.
When nightmares have ended
And blue skies are warming,
While deep in my garden
There's petal-cups forming.

Am I the woman ...
Who when owls are flying
You'll hurry home to me
With love undenying.
At dusk cold and lonely
There'll be no more crying
For I am the woman
To love 'til you're dying.

Our Dream House

There is a house within our dreams, mid fields of wheat and rye,
So tranquilly it waits for us, this house, we'd love to buy -
It slumbers in a copper wood bright as a polished jewel,
Which needs to be reset in gold for rebirth and renewal.

This house that's nestling in a vale is kissed by sloping hills,
Where cattle hug surrounding fields beyond pale daffodils.
Such joy I know should fill this house with laughter, love and care,
Someone to bring it back to life, with happiness to spare.

This house we've travelled long to find is statuesque and grand,
Yet lain so empty these past years just waiting for my hand
And by the weeping willow tree, a lovely wooden seat,
That's wide enough to cuddle you and rest our weary feet.

This house, we'll fill with furniture and fabrics in rich hues,
Brocades with silks and velveteens, 'neath ornate curlicues.
We'll cast a spell upon this house to let the sun seep through,
Upon the floors of polished oak and doors of palest yew.

This house should be awash with flowers on tops ashine with wax,
Wild marguerites, picked on our walk arranged with golden flax,
And when the moon is riding high, these pleasures we shall own,
To watch the sunset sink below no ruin - but our home.

I'll Look Around

Somewhere a lovely garden waits for me,
with ancient vines and trees extraordinaire,
where on a summer's day
when dreams are far away,
I'll look around and know that you are there.

A garden facing out towards the sea,
where I can sit with sunlight in my hair
and when the seagulls call
to warn me of a squall
I'll look around and know that you are there.

There is a cottage by a lonely beach,
with rocks where I may clamber without care,
when kissing waves embrace
a rainbow giving chase
I'll look around and know that you are there.

A cottage with a rose around the door,
where peonies will bloom most everywhere
and when I hear your feet
on stairs echoing sweet
I'll look around and know that you are there.

There is a garden gate to lead me to,
a door that opens to this cottage where,
my happiness will lie
until the day I die,
I'll look around and know that you are there.

If Only

If only you were here today
In Paradise with me,
To watch the sun rise from her bed
While pelicans fly overhead -
As dolphins leap around the bay
For half the sky to see;
If only you were here today
In Paradise with me.

If only you were in my sight
I could forget to weep,
Across this sparkling stretch of Isle,
Where combers roll for mile on mile
Upon the shoreline creamy white
Where loveliness won't sleep;
If only you were in my sight
I could forget to weep.

If only I could take your hand
Beneath this half of sky,
Where curling waves around our feet,
As white as snow are calling sweet
Upon the rocks and shifting sand
As palm trees softly sigh;
If only I could take your hand
Beneath this half of sky.

If only I could kiss your lips
And hold you to my breast,
To see the golden sun go down,
To walk with you without a frown
Before the moon with magic flips
As shadows softly rest;
If only I could kiss your lips
And hold you to my breast.

The Little Folk (Muses)

There are so many little folk
Who live inside my head,
While some are sad, some like a joke,
A few fill me with dread.

One takes me over field and dell
To maybe chase white deer,
Or over bridges by Brunel
Of whom there's no compeer.

Of course there's one who makes me wish
For things I haven't got,
Like cocktail gowns in silks that swish,
And cruises on a yacht.

One makes me dream of years gone by
To times when I was sad,
To when I used to wonder why
I had the life I had.

Of course there's one who makes me see
The storms of snow that rage.
Who bids me dance in Neptune's sea,
With metaphors to wage.

These little folk who bounce around
Say words I can't ignore,
One told me of a fairy mound
With magic to explore.

One made me write of marching feet
And then a red beret,
He urged a soldier's brave heartbeat,
I penned without delay.

In haste I write of plants in bloom
And early morning dew,
And my dream house within a coomb,
Because they tell me to.

At times they get it awf'lly wrong
which leads to bad critique,
They mess about the whole daylong
with odes not quite sapphic.

I'm forced to write of love's desire
And kisses sweet as wine,
Of one who sets my heart afire
And in whose eyes I shine.

They whisper to me night and day,
At all hours of the clock,
Demanding that I must obey,
Detering writer's block!

A Valentine Promise

Here's the land of milk and honey, you promised long ago
With the moon slow serenading as Cupid found his bow,
On a February evening, while sipping ice-chilled wine
When you promised me forever to be my Valentine.

Here's the paradise you promised, as I recall we kissed
In the soft caress of starlight before the morning mist,
On a February evening, when all the world seemed fine
When I promised you forever to be your Valentine.

Here's the poetry I promised, with twilight in my eyes
When the snow was falling softly beneath romantic skies,
On a February evening, when all the world was mine
When we toasted one another, A Happy Valentine.

Because Of You

Because of you I wake each morn
and rise to meet the day,
to see the world in different hues
in every known which way.
I never get enough of you,
my old age I'll postpone,
for love I never thought I'd have,
for love I've never known.

Because of you my days reach out
to share so many things,
such as our love of poetry
with joy each stanza brings.
The touch of hands to spark a kiss
whenever we're alone,
such love I never thought I'd have,
such love I've never known.

Because of you my nights are sweet
as honey from the bee,
as 'neath the beauty of the stars
you pledge your love to me.
To see desire within your eyes
reflecting in my own,
with love I never thought I'd have,
with love I've never known.

Ask Not

Ask not how we shall love from now,
It's written in the stars
And in each song of love we hear,
Strummed softly by guitars.
Nor ask me as I fall asleep
If my heart is but true,
Because I'll have to tell you this,
I'll give my life for you.

Ask not if my heart beats as yours,
The willows whisper so,
As will the moon in velvet skies
Cast you a silv'ry glow.
And ask me not through veils of rain
If kisses taste like wine,
For when we kiss I tell the world
That darling you are mine.

Ask not when strolling hand in hand
Through poppies in a field,
If for eternity we'll love
As harvests surely yield.
Nor ask with laughter at twilight
As rainbows kiss the day,
If I will stay as close to you,
As you to me, I pray.

Ask not how we shall love from now,
We'll find a way my love ....somehow.
~~~ 🌹 ~~~

For Georgie

Through mem'ry's door I wander
To see my babe once more,
To read a bedtime story
Cross-legged upon the floor,
Surrounded by her playthings
I'm reading of a land,
Where knights will joust for kingdoms
To win a maiden's hand.

She giggles when I mention
How fairies fly between,
Each sycamore and willow
To paint four shades of green,
And how the pixies gather
In gowns of tulle and lace,
To pirouette in summer
When stars with moon embrace.

Now snug beneath her blanket
And Granma's knitted shawl,
To soothe her baby nightmares
Should any come to call,
I hate to leave this mem'ry
But now my babe is grown,
And telling her own stories
To children of her own ....

I Won't Deny

I think I'll build my life again
And venture from this city,
I'm sure it's just as nice elsewhere
And hopefully as pretty.
I'll not deny some things I'll miss, such as my garden which is bliss,
Or walks with friends without a care
With secrets only girls can share.

I know I'll miss my climbing rose,
How tall it always towers,
Where everyone can see the mass
Of lovely perfumed flowers.
I can't deny I'll miss the view but now my dreams are coming true,
With blossoms round a cottage door
Where only weeds have grown before.

I'll take my fav'rite things with me
And cuttings from the garden,
Where hopefully they'll bloom in time,
If not, I'll beg your pardon.
I won't deny that once or twice I may look back and in a trice
Recall a mem'ry here and there
And say, 'do you remember where?'

My life with you I'll build again
And have no trouble trying,
The last piece of the jigsaw's here,
It fits, there's no decrying.
I shan't deny that in my dreams you've always been there, so it seems -
My future now will start anew,
When Spring is here .... I'll be with you.

The Wine Was Sweet

The wine was sweet upon his lips I kissed so tenderly,
beneath what seemed a moon eclipsed especially for me,
across the lake where dimly slips a shadow clearly free.
Such memories shall stay within my heart.

The whisper of a firefly beneath the willows bent,
disturbed only a peaceful sigh, undoubtedly content,
before the dawn awoke the sky after the night was spent.
Such memories shall stay within my heart.

The star that danced for our delight, so cool and so serene,
just as the beauty of the night saw moths of shining green
and drooping wings in gentle flight skimming the lakes between.
Such memories shall stay within my heart.

The fish were silent, blowing cold, as birds in chorus sang,
while coots and ducklings, ever bold, crossed fishing lines that rang,
and yet we sat for hours untold, loving the whole shebang.
Such memories shall stay within my heart.

The magic of time standing still for us to sit awhile
to watch late summer drift until the autumn gave a smile,
upon the softly curving hill where hawks flew single file.
Such memories shall stay within my heart.

The castle where we had cream tea before an open fire,
seated with graciousness at three with antiques to admire,
where Kings and Queens through history had dined in fine attire.
Such memories shall stay within my heart.

Will You Love Me

Will you love me as the blackbirds slow waken from their sleep,
when frost lays cold upon the ground as winter slumbers deep
or in the warming rays of sun when finches harvest fruit,
for their pretty newborn chicks in my old discarded boot?

Will you love me in a rainstorm that lasts the whole day long,
when out of tune I sing for you a silly ragtime song;
while yet again you cook for me with garlic and red wine,
with not a care for anything...especially my waistline?

Will you love me when I laugh with a tear here in my eye,
when your idiotic joke makes my breath skip on a sigh
or when we dance beneath the moon ashimmer with delight,
before we pour a nightcap, kissing tenderly goodnight?

Will you love me every springtime for all of evermore,
when the bluebells smell delicious upon the forest floor
and sycamores don every shade of green in every hue
and songbirds tell me once again that I'm in love with you?

Some Days

Some days are turquoise,
Some are pink
With lipstick red to make boys wink,
And stockings, silken,
Black as night,
When feeling frivolously bright..

You'd be surprised how many times,
My colours change to write in rhymes.

It Happened Not In Summer

It was not on a summer's day
Our loving die was cast;
It was the chill of wintertime,
With snowflakes falling fast.

For me a season without hope,
Yet when I saw you there,
I knew we'd love before the spring
When blossoms filled the air.

And as you held my hand in yours
I knew our love would last;
It was the chill of wintertime,
With snowflakes falling fast.

At twilight when we said goodbye
I kissed you in full view,
Of passing strangers who could see
My dreams were coming true.

I oft' recall when first we met -
With milestones we have passed;
Long since that chill of wintertime,
When snowflakes fell so fast.

Much Laughter In The Air

The restaurant was busy with much laughter in the air,
the night she sat beside him in the 'Bistro Chantaclaire.'
They'd spent the day sightseeing, for this meeting was their first,
and now sought refuge for a meal with drinks to quench their thirst.
She told him over salmon mousse how she had lived her life,
regaling him with anecdotes of happiness and strife,
and how she'd been afraid to meet someone she barely knew –
when he suggested meeting 'neath the clock at Waterloo.
But now she knew she'd love this man with ev'ry waking hour,
and suddenly a nightingale woke in his leafy bower.

The restaurant was busy with much laughter in the air,
the night she sat beside him in the 'Bistro Chantaclaire.'
A dozen times they'd eaten here but still felt like the first,
each time his hand caressed her own she felt her heart would burst.
He told her over entrecotes' how much she meant to him,
she was the very air he breathed, his every working limb,
with not a moment passing that he didn't think of her,
she cried hot stinging tears and his face became a blur.
She knew though without seeing there was stardust in his eyes,
and suddenly a nightingale looked to the moonlit skies.

The restaurant was busy with much laughter in the air,
the night they sat together in the 'Bistro Chantaclaire.'
A hundred times they'd eaten here and still he held her hand,
so beautifully manicured but older now and tanned.
She told him over Torte Limone how happy she had been,
and how her love was still as strong as all the years between
and as they gazed towards the skies bedazzled by moonbeams
they thanked a million stars for fulfilling all their dreams.
The restaurant was busy with much laughter in the air,
When suddenly a nightingale sang for this grand affair.

One Day

One day when I'm out riding and with friends perhaps confiding,
is that the day my love will come for me?
When I'm feeling kinda lonesome, forlorn or on my ownsome,
I'll see him looking handsome and carefree.

Or perhaps when I'm snowballing when everything's enthralling,
as snowflakes fall so even, crisp and sweet.
When swans fly proudly overhead eager for their nesting bed,
I'll see him tread where snowdrops bloom discreet.

Maybe when I'm star gazing at the heavens so amazing,
beneath the willow, weeping in the night,
When the moon drifts ever high to kiss the purple of the sky,
I'll hear his voice call soft within my sight..

It could be early morning with a saffron sun adorning,
in springtime, restless summer or the fall.
Or when I read my latest book over by the babbling brook,
maybe I'll see him standing there so tall.

Or as I lay daydreaming with my sleepy head a scheming,
within my garden in the midst of June.
Before sipping cocoa I'll hear his footstep and I'll know,
at last, he's here and I'm over the moon.

.... One day!

Blind Date

Upon the day I met him there were people passing by,
  all going who knows where without a smile.
While waiting on the station feeling introvert and shy,
  I searched in every face at the turnstile.

The seconds turned to minutes as I wondered, should I go,
  was this a great mistake I would regret.
As trains were hissing wildly I then heard a whistle blow,
  maybe I ought to wait a while... and yet.

It was then I saw him through a veil of shining tears,
  a mirage in soft undulating sand.
But as he walked towards me he washed away the years
  and smiling broad he held my soft, warm hand.

I had never seen a rainbow until the day we met,
  nor seen a flame of autumn on a tree.
But here I was eyes gleaming, dancing a pirouette
  whilst feeling liberated and carefree.

Since then each day is summer and all the world is warm
  and kissing is in season all the year.
Today my heart's a mountainside, free of rains that storm,
  as I ascend, no longer do I fear.

I Have Love (Triolet)

I feel your kiss against my own
And sigh with wonder at your touch,
You smell divine with musk cologne,
I feel your kiss against my own.
No longer must I stand alone
For I have love within my clutch,
I feel your kiss against my own
And sigh with wonder at your touch.

After The Rain

Before the hour I kissed you,
before the dawn grew light,
a gentle rain fell softly
to glisten crystal-white,
upon my wide veranda
where breezes serenade,
with millions of voices
to herald rain's cascade.

After the hour I kissed you,
after you'd said goodbye,
the cool-soft grey of rain clouds
in mourning rolled on by,
and from my wide veranda
'neath skies of pigeon-blue,
I saw the earth anointed
and thought, only of you.

Poetry In Motion

You are poetry in motion within my repertoire -
A ballade in the spotlight with a certain je ne quoi,
You're the rosebud 'neath the arbour still blooming without fail,
The tea-set on the dresser and the hammer to my nail,
You're the tissue when I'm sneezing teased gently from the box
When day equals the night-time at the point of equinox,
You're the brave, triumphant chorus of dawn awakened birds
And the diction'ry I'm searching, for long-forgotten words.

You're my Romeo beseeching below the balcony,
When the moon is sailing higher for lovers such as we,
You're the marzipan and icing and ribbon round the cake
When again I'm one year older with time to merry-make,
You're my anchor firmly grounded beneath the ocean's roar,
I'm the mermaid swimming round you, in love, and furthermore
You're the bacon in my sandwich and sugar in my tea,
With a smile that I adore, sweet as honey from the bee.

You're the light when day is dawning and psalm at evensong,
You're my Derby to my Joan holding me the whole night long,
You're the prayer to God said daily, imploring you stay well,
You're tomatoes in my omelette and heather on the fell,
In the golden rays of autumn when breezes lisp a chill
You're the raindrops falling gently, my spirit and my will;
You're the blossom in the pear tree the north wind blew away
.....But here you are my darling and I held you close today.

I'd Love To Dance

I'd love to dance with you tonight,
To feel your cheek against my own,
When silver moonbeams are in sight
I'd love to dance with you tonight.
Before my hair becomes too white
And I forget the dreams I've known,
I'd love to dance with you tonight,
To feel your cheek against my own.

I'd love to dance within your arms,
In moon glow falling from the sky,
Beneath the magic of your charms,
I'd love to dance within your arms.
Perhaps to Chopin, Liszt or Brahms
Before my time arrives to die,
I'd love to dance within your arms
In moon glow falling from the sky

I'd love to dance with you once more,
Just once before the fiddler flees,
Just once before the last encore,
I'd love to dance with you once more.
Perhaps within the ocean's roar
Of her sweet calling harmonies,
I'd love to dance with you once more,
Just once before the fiddler flees.

Love (Monotetra)

They fell in love a while ago,
While eating in a small bistro,
Paella with a fine merlot
And then cointreau and then cointreau.

And when they kissed, it felt so right,
Beneath the moon glistening white,
To say they wished to re-unite,
Another night, another night.

Such memories they have to share,
Of lover's trysts without despair,
With walks through town and country air,
And all that's there and all that's there.

Now five full years have almost passed,
Some folk declared it wouldn't last,
But their love's stronger and steadfast,
The die is cast, the die is cast.

'One day,' they always seem to sigh
While dreaming, gazing to the sky,
'We'll be together, you and I,
Before we die, before we die.

Sisters

My hair was gold as summer corn,
my sister's amber-flame,
born early on a Pisces morn
in spring, past winter's frame.

Fond mem'ries I share with her
to bind our hearts afresh -
where kindness needs a comforter,
each knot I'll tie with mesh.

My blood, my tears, my sister kin,
our lives have slow unfurled
to see our daughters' lives begin
through *us* to face *their* world.

My hair's now silver like the moon
my sister's *still* aflame,
still singing melodies in tune
in spring, past winter's frame.

Memories

They sip a sparkling chardonnay remembering when young,
warm summers surfing oceans on a dare,
when stars were at their best dressed by the honey coloured-moon
while fireflies were dancing everywhere.

The ancient castle stood aloft beyond the southern downs,
as they recall their honeymoon spent there,
in autumn as the leaves turned gold and loveliness was theirs,
while fireflies were dancing everywhere.

Now bathing in the moonfire glow the stars blot out the day,
to cast a glint upon his silv'ry hair,
while memories of babes in arms are softly brought to mind,
when fireflies were dancing everywhere.

Beneath the pureness of the sky they memorise each kiss,
more tender than a wisp of maidenhair,
as moonlight chequers silver to enchant the atmosphere
and fireflies are dancing everywhere.

Recalling 'neath the sycamore their marriage long ago,
when all of nature seemed extraordinaire,
yet with each chink of memory they know there'll always be
the fireflies *still* dancing everywhere.

Crack Of Dawn

As dawn peers round the corner where the mist swirls grey and deep,
the moon's slow disappearing from the sky.
While in the far-off distance there's the whistle from a train,
as mallards with their young fly ever high.
I reach to pull the covers up and wonder to myself
what fate decrees to greet this summer day.
Will I stay a moment longer, while musing in the warmth,
or rise to chase the cats with morning prey?

The moon has made its journey to the far side of the world
and stars have followed on within its sight,
while deep within my garden walls I heard the echoes call,
as wild things stalked their victims through the night.
I see the curtains waver in the early morning breeze
and wonder if the larks are on the wing.
Will I stay a moment longer, while musing in the warmth,
or rise to feed the blackbirds as they sing?

Though scarce ten minutes now have passed and here's the paperboy,
he's whistling as he turns into the lane.
I see the mist still floating and the street lamp shining through,
as I embrace my feather counterpane.
The day has dawned in glory for my blossoms to unfurl
where dragonflies will soar on wings of lace.
Will I stay a moment longer, while musing in the warmth,
or turn to kiss my darling's handsome face?

Our Love

Our love is like the sweetest rose,
Pale as the snow it gently grows
To soft entwine and then enclose
My heart with everything.

And like the rose I reach so high
Yet never do I wish to fly,
Away from you or question why
My heart with anything.

The sun will flood our souls until
The rose no longer blooms to thrill,
Yet love will surely over-fill
My heart without warning.

Yes, love is like a web slow spun,
Between each petal one by one,
In morning mist or thereupon
My heart with comforting.

I cherish each and every day
Love proves sorrow can drift away
And who am I to disobey
My heart so now trusting.

Love's gentle as a summer breeze
And I have feelings such as these,
Where there's no reason to appease
My heart with anything.

We Need To Talk

We need to talk regarding many things,
of winters past, yet still a host of springs;
when daffodils will in a crescent sprawl,
and grasses eager start to grow so tall.

We need to see afar beyond our eyes,
sweet roses scattered 'neath translucent skies,
or sunlight pouring gold on fields of corn
for birds with wings that beat in early dawn.

We need our love to guide us through the years,
and yet be not afraid to shroud our tears,
when hand in hand we'll cast for dreams in sight
beneath a distant moon in sequined night.

We need to talk regarding many things:
of winters, summers, falls and joyous springs.

I See You Everywhere

I see you everywhere I look
And in each love song I revere
In magazine and story book
I see you everywhere I look
In each and every crannied nook
Your face is smiling crystal clear
I see you everywhere I look
And in each love song I revere

Pearls Of Rain

Supple and slim in ev'ry limb,
Ablaze with warm desire,
Fine lace perfumes, wholly consumes
A flame that won't expire.

Beneath the stars we think are ours,
Ashine like molten gold,
A naked touch can prove too much,
As loving hours unfold.

Soft tears again like pearls of rain,
Glimpsed through a mist at sea,
I see a smile and for a while
There's only you and me.

With swaying hips and kissing lips
As sweet as sugar spun,
And whisp'ring sighs into veiled eyes
Say, 'you're the only one.'

Til Break Of Day

She will not close her eyes tonight,
She'll dance 'til break of day,
Until the moon has lost its light
And stars have cast away.
Her gown leaves neck and shoulders bare,
In palest gold to match her hair
And as the music fills the air,
She feels her body sway.
There's nothing she has ever seen
As beautiful as this,
In gowns of white and blue and green
Each lady hopes to kiss -
Beneath the moon in star-filled skies,
There's romance sparkling in their eyes,
In shadows deep where fireflies,
Can scarce not go amiss.

She will not close her eyes tonight,
She'll dance a waltz by Strauss
And foxtrot to her heart's delight,
Within this grand old house.
She'll drift immortal, sweet and young,
To dance on air with arms up-flung,
With pleasures up to now unsung,
Or ardour yet to douse.
There's no-one she has ever seen
As handsome as her beau
And nothing ever comes between
Her love for him, you know.
So in her gown of golden lace
She waltzes with him face to face.
She knows there is no other place,
 Within the moonshine's glow
She will not close her eyes tonight ....

With Sadness....

Meadow View

I'm on a desert Island; I've been here countless years,
Dreaming of horizons new through soft abandoned tears.
'They' said things would improve if I came to 'Meadow View,'
'They' said my house was big for me, what I need's, 'bijou.'
Now countless days I sit here, just waiting, all alone,
Alas, *'They'* never visit, nor do *'They'* telephone.

I'm on a desert Island; Been here for countless years,
Beneath a palm tree swaying through soft abandoned tears.
My upright chair's a hammock, to ease my aching back,
My bath with handles either side's my little red kayak.
Sometimes I glimpse a passing ship, 'ahoy' I cry, 'who's there,
Please won't you come ashore today, *please,* pull up a chair?'

I'm on a desert Island; *marooned* here countless years,
Dreaming of eternity, through soft abandoned tears.
I have a nice Girl Friday who's from MacMillan's Trust,
She giggles when I tell her my thoughts of wanderlust.
But tells me it's not long now, because that passing ship
Is just offshore at anchor and waits my final trip.

I'll leave this desert island, I've been here many years,
I'm now going to Paradise, where God will dry my tears....

Follow the Hearse

We follow on behind the hearse,
This swine flu has become a curse,
We hope and pray it won't be us
The hearse calls for with pomp and fuss.
You'll be picked up then lowered down
While kith and kin stand all around.
They'll throw a sod and mouth a prayer
And look with tears towards your heir.

They'll cover you with cold, damp earth,
And friends that you have known from birth
Will hug for comfort with a kiss,
While some may even be speechless.
Then to the wake they'll all retreat,
To drink your wine and meet and greet
Friends you never knew you had
And shaking heads whisper, 'how sad.'

Some will bestow an accolade,
Maybe relate an escapade,
Then say, 'how kind and nice you were,'
Fond memories they will bestir.
And meanwhile deep within your box -
Amongst the soil and clay and rocks,
The beetles and the worms move in
To visit your silk lined coffin.

Your teeth fall in and your eyes drop out
And you'll get thin instead of stout,
Before too long you'll look like hell -
Within this box where you now dwell.
Quite soon the angels shall appear
To tell you, not to worry dear;
Your soul has gone for God to keep
So in his hands, you can now sleep.

My Silent Childhood

When I was young there were no trees,
I don't remember soft warm knees
Or any kindness in a voice,
Or any song that would rejoice.

My father would bellow and cry
But as a child I knew not why,
His temper always on the boil,
He too was deaf, so in turmoil.

My mother also cried a lot
But somehow didn't give a jot,
I don't remember arms that cared,
Only bad moods with nostrils flared.

My playmate was a big 'black dog,'
Not for me, dolls or leapfrog -
A hand that slapped and caused me pain,
My parents arguing again.

No-one but no-one seemed to care
As I trembled behind a chair,
The 'black dog' sitting on my knee,
The only one to care for me.

Within my silent world I cried,
But no-one ever once replied.

Perhaps In Winter

I'll seek His presence one day
When life is past its best,
Maybe at dawn with birdsong
Or twilight, when they rest.

Or when the springtime's over
With blossoms blown away,
When summer flees to autumn
As grasses turn to hay.

A calm there'll be about me
To see His presence there,
When days of wine and roses
Leave me to bow in prayer.

I'll linger for a moment,
To kiss, smile, then depart,
With all my labours resting
And peace within my heart.

At last I'll know the secret
Of His divinity,
When faith kneels by me gladly,
As death calls soft to me.

What Shall I Do?

What shall I do my darling, when
the winter comes by us again,
when all the garden's fast asleep
and creatures are in burrows deep.
When violets no longer bloom
and rose mislays her own perfume,
when one by one the leaves fall down
revealing winter's thorn-filled crown.
When rivers iced no longer stream
so can't reflect a sweet moonbeam,
when there's no sign of sun nor thaw
and I still miss you ... more and more.

When golden days are black as night
to hide the sun from my delight,
or when the birds no longer sing,
newborn and sweet and wondering
and I'm left here, frozen, alone,
older and wrinkled to the bone
as thunder strikes with veils of rain
to lash against my windowpane -
as with a flood of tears I weep
each day I wake from restless sleep,
when snow is two feet at my door
and I still miss you ... more and more.

What shall I do my darling?

Poem full Of Chimes

When the clock was chiming early
On the day my babe was born,
With her golden hair so curly,
Like a field of ripened corn.
I could see the future clearly,
I could see how she would fare,
I could see my own sweet baby
With a smile to light a flare.

When the clock was chiming later
As the school bell rang aloud,
I sang praise to my creator
For I'd never been so proud.
I could hear the blackbirds' chorus,
I could hear the alphabet,
I could hear the heartbreak calling
For her first major regret.

When the clock chimed ever after,
On her wedding day of bliss,
There was love and joyous laughter
As she placed her hand in his.
I could feel her love surround me,
I could feel her heartbeat fast,
I could feel happy tomorrows
As those memories were cast.

Now the clock's no longer chiming,
All I have's a photograph
And this poem full of rhyming
To remind me of her laugh.
I can cry a trillion tears,
I can cry 'til next July,
I can cry beyond my lifetime
Or until the seas run dry.

Without You

I sleep with you and wake with you,
In mem'ries you are there,
My dreams are full of thoughts of you
With nothing to compare,
Your eyes I see beseeching me
Alas, you're not in sight
But you're the one I yearn to see,
Throughout each hour of night.

I wandered through my day's routine
With hopes to do my best,
I danced alone to our beguine
And held you to my breast.
Without you I know only fear,
So think of other things
But like a childhood thought my dear,
Your memory just clings.

Your love bathed me in golden sun
With shelter from each storm,
At last I had somewhere to run
With you to keep me warm,
To stay forever close to me -
As dawn is to the dew,
As nectar's to the honey bee,
As flowers are to Kew.

I sleep with you and wake with you
And sometimes you *are* there.

Thoughts at Twilight

At twilight when the sun has dimmed
and all the earth smells damp and sweet,
she peers above the water's edge,
to feel the wind beneath her feet.
  Where shadows spread and gently stir,
  and only crickets sing to her.

This is a very magic place -
with beauty you have never seen,
where hawks fly proudly overhead
and egrets on the bank convene.
  Where shadows spread and gently stir,
  and only crickets sing to her.

As she remembers blissful days
alone, her mem'ries start to cry,
there's much of him to think about
when swallows circle in the sky.
  Where shadows spread and gently stir,
  and only crickets sing to her.

He used to stand here with his arm
around her waist at close of day,
to listen to the curlew's wail
on wings that swoop in search of prey.
  Where shadows spread and gently stir,
  and only crickets sing to her.

His smile is everywhere she looks
but that which makes her cry the most,
is knowing she will only see
him stand before her as a ghost.
  Where shadows spread and gently stir,
  only the crickets sing to her.

A Life No More

My past life is but mine no more,
It's ravaged to the inner core.
The years and hours now almost gone
In flames, a veil of fine chiffon.

Alone I stand with tearful eyes,
Afraid to lift them to the skies.
Dark searing pain tears at my soul,
As for my life I take control.

Whatever will become of me?
I cry and clasp my hands to plea,
So old to start my life anew,
To seek new love forever true.

But by a miracle I find,
A heart with vows to fill my mind,
We'll toil each second and some more,
To fit the last piece of jigsaw.

If Only

If only you were here today
In Paradise with me,
To watch the sun rise from her bed
While pelicans fly overhead -
As dolphins leap around the bay
For half the sky to see;
If only you were here today
In Paradise with me.

If only you were in my sight
I could forget to weep,
Across this sparkling stretch of Isle,
Where combers roll for mile on mile
Upon the shoreline creamy white
Where loveliness won't sleep;
If only you were in my sight
I could forget to weep.

If only I could take your hand
Beneath this half of sky,
Where curling waves around our feet,
As white as snow are calling sweet
Upon the rocks and shifting sand
As palm trees softly sigh;
If only I could take your hand
Beneath this half of sky.

If only I could kiss your lips
And hold you to my breast,
To see the golden sun go down,
To walk with you without a frown
Before the moon with magic flips
As shadows softly rest;
If only I could kiss your lips
And hold you to my breast.

Below Par

Why does today seem far away,
It hovers out of reach,
My soul seems dead like cold grey lead
As barren as my speech.

From mists of pearl that gently swirl
Around my aching head,
The hours unfold so uncontrolled
Are filling me with dread.

Such loneliness for a caress
Brings to my eye a tear,
To spill upon like fine chiffon
My heartache so severe.

But then I see a galaxy
Of beauty in the night,
A shining moon to make me swoon
And dance for his delight.

Will I

What is it like to be so old,
alone with no-one there to hold.
Will ev'ry hour of ev'ry day
be spent dreaming of 'faraway.'
Will I no longer style my hair
because I have less need to care.
Will people shout and ridicule
and think of me a damned old fool.
Will I still jive to rock 'n' roll
or slow foxtrot to Nat King Cole.
Will I still sing 'As Time Goes By'
(will fundamental things apply).
Is there a future there to see
or will it be twiddle-dee-dee.
Will I forget here, now, today
with folks I've met along the way

Will I sit in a pinafore
where once I only wore Dior,
or will it matter what I wear
upon my fattened derriere.
I s'pect I'll eat past 'sell by date,'
or worse lose weight and de-hydrate
and will I have to leave my home
because I have some weird syndrome.
Will I no longer walk my dogs
across the Lammas, through the bogs
to meet with friends along the way
for coffee in a small cafe.
......And will I dream the whole day long
of my one love that was so strong
with passion that I cannot waive
Thus, I will take him to my grave.
Will I ?........
Please God, I won't.

Reconcile

She had not meant to fall asleep,
Only to rest a little while,
For over hill and golden vale
She'd walked with hopes of reconcile.
Towards the stream where slender ferns
lay clustered close beneath the shade,
And through the pine trees in between
The churchyard nestling in the glade.

Beyond the beach with yellow sand
Where foaming crests roll to the shore,
With shells of pink and purple hues
And gulls and terns in loud rapport.
She ran to meet the water's edge,
Her eyes amist with crystal tears
And as the ocean called to her
She thought of all the wasted years.

Once there was passion in his eyes
When happiness was theirs to share,
And when he kissed her curving lips
She'd float on clouds above the air.
The ocean stroked her gleaming throat,
As once again she felt his breath
And felt his love envelop her,
As real to her as her own death.

She saw the church come into view
With peals calling for evensong
And then the stream with slender ferns,
Had she been gone the whole day long?
She had not meant to fall asleep,
Only to rest a little while
For over hill and golden vale,
He brought her home to reconcile.

Men From Nowhere

He came from nowhere, out of sight
With eyes intent on harm,
She screamed and putting up a fight
He shook her to be calm.
Then roughly forced her to the ground,
While others quickly tightly bound,
  To keep her still
  To keep her still
And silence her with scarves that wound.

Her eyes with terror stared at stars
And at the moon now dim,
And was that smell of stale cigars
On shirts of blue denim.
They laughed and ridiculed each thrust
With sickening enraging lust,
  Their mocking scorn
  Their mocking scorn
Made her repulsive with disgust.

Her body, they rolled to and fro
Upon the ground so cold,
And someone in a red bandeau
Had her in stranglehold.
And all the while they drank whisky,
While getting evermore frisky,
  With no escape
  With no escape
From their merciless savagery.

And then their laughter was no more
As silence filled the air,
With eyes that wept and broken jaw
And body bruised and bare.
A broken doll near death, in pain,

Impregnated by men, insane,
  Then left to die
  Then left to die
Another victim of cocaine!

All night she lay beside death's door,
Until a passer-by,
Saw her beneath the prickly haw
While trembling with a sigh.
What animals could do this deed?
To leave her here to weep and bleed
  To die in pain
  To die in pain
Beside a field of gold rapeseed.

When He Returns (Monotetra)

Her skin is golden as the shore,
With neither blemish nor a flaw,
On his return he'll gaze in awe,
When back from war, when back from war.

And in his arms she'll gently lay,
While in their dreams they'll castaway,
To love where palm trees softly sway
And dolphins play and dolphins play.

They'll be no talk of things aghast,
Or missions solemnly broadcast,
Of comrades who have died too fast,
By bombs that blast, by bombs that blast.

At noon she got the telegram,
'Killed on patrol by Taliban,'
Now she's alone without her man,
Afghanistan, Afghanistan.

Little Beaver

'Cross the plains of Oklahoma
You will hear a folklore tale,
Of a brave called Little Beaver,
For his magic they'll regale.
You will hear his name in lodges,
On the prairies, hot and dry,
In the wigwams of the chieftains
Telling trappers passing by.

While the elders of the nation
Who no longer ride to wars,
Will narrate of Little Beaver
To papooses of young squaws.
You will hear he's a brave hunter
With a spirit in his veins,
From across loud rushing rivers,
To the dry sequestered plains.

Far beyond the plains the forests,
With jade pine trees growing tall,
They will talk about his exploits,
From the spring through to the fall.
They will speak of warring parties
And the visions he foresaw,
Of forthcoming wars of nations,
'Neath the flight of the condor.

He saw dangers in a crystal,
That he wore next to his heart
And with hissing from winged serpents,
Such dangers he could impart.
For two sunsets Little Beaver
Gazed into his crystal heart
To foresee a trail of tears,
Where the mountain ranges start.

So he called the tribes to council
And with wisdom spoke in peace,
Telling of the hissing serpents
With their wings of deep cerise.
From the Mississippi river
They would trek one thousand miles,
Little Beaver saw it clearly
When he saw the corpse stockpiles.

And some rode on mustang ponies
And some walked a darkened haze
Far beneath the eyes of eagles,
Where the bison freely graze
And the spirits looked upon them
As they smoked their pipes of peace,
As they smoked the pipes together,
Free of any war-paint grease.

And they marched with lack of water,
Overland and to the west
And they died in tens of thousands,
With their loved ones to their breast
And they said, farewell to rivers,
Where the fish were plentiful
And the land of their forefathers,
Where beauty was visible.

'Cross the plains of Oklahoma,
You will see the Cherokees
And you'll hear of Little Beaver
With his tragic prophesies.
You will also hear from Pawnee,
Kickapoos and Chickasaws,
Starved and beaten from their homelands
Exiled from their southern shores....

Reflections On The Shore

She feels she has to walk alone,
To gather thoughts, with hair windblown,
Maybe the breeze will blow away
Her cares and woes of this past day.
As clouds of silver race on by,
The breeze picks up and with a sigh,
She wonders where it all went wrong,
Could she perhaps, have been more strong.

Yet looking back along the shore
There's nature's beauty without flaw,
With hills rolling to meet the sand,
As breeze 'pon breeze blows each hair strand.
The sparkling foam from off the sea
Slows down her pace to some degree,
With sunshine warm against her skin
Now burning, much to her chagrin.

Her freckles will come out to play
To seem like caramel frappe,
Then turn a softly golden hue,
The colour of a pale bamboo.
She should go home for tea with him
And not act like the poor victim,
To share that smile he longs to see
While saying, 'darling, I'm sorry.'

He'll take her soft warm hand in his,
Perhaps pick up two wine glasses
And with his arm around her waist,
They'll climb the stairs, with urgent haste!

Diary of a Call girl

It's just another Sunday night
With tricks to turn before daylight,
I've rent to pay and kids to feed
And now my mum's an invalid.

It's just another Monday night
I'm sent to tease and then delight,
Some want it quick, some want it slow,
I do what's asked and then I go.

It's just another Tuesday night
I hope to God I'll be alright,
Last night a girl was badly beat
And from a car thrown on the street.

It's just another Wednesday night
And business men need to ignite
Some thrills with pleasure to their lives,
You'd think they'd go home to their wives.

It's just another Thursday night
Just one to go, a socialite,
Who sits by day in Parliament,
By night debauched and decadent.

It's just another Friday night
I'll kindle passions to excite
Men with whom I've no rapport,
Old men who like to call me whore!

It's just another working night,
When will I dance beneath moonlight?

In The Nursery ....

New Arrival

Hush my baby, hush my baby,
Brush away your tears of pearl
'Pon your cheeks softer than cotton,
My own lovely baby girl.
Who's the fairest, who's the fairest,
You shall dance where'er you be
On a star near glist'ning moonbeams,
Singing soft a melody.

Hush sweet baby, hush sweet baby,
Nymphs arrive to cast a spell,
Floating on a breeze of ermine,
Paler than a cockle-shell.
Now you're smiling, now you're smiling,
Can you hear the lullaby -
Whispered from a thousand angels
Way above the clouds so high.

Hush my baby, hush my baby,
Drift where there's no sound nor sigh,
To the land of milk and honey
Far beyond this half of sky.
Here's the sandman, here's the sandman,
On a cloud of crystal-white,
Go with him my own sweet baby,
God bless always through the night.

I'll Bring You Fairytales

Come sit, it's time for fairytales
From this my book of rhyme,
I'll take you to a land of dreams
Where clocks don't tell the time,
More distant than you've ever been
Where stories will unfold,
Of tigers, mice and butterflies
And unicorns of olde.

With hands outstretched you'll need to touch
The beauty all around -
Yet should you be so well inclined
There's magic to be found,
In kingdoms ruled each by a King
With Queens sat by their side,
Where jousting Knights fight for the hands
Of maidens, misty-eyed.

While dragons roam with fiery breath,
Green caterpillars sing
To wake the dormouse from her sleep
As winter turns to spring.
And then upon another page
A moth's slow drifting by,
To warn of witches within sight
On broomsticks flying high.

Tooth fairies by the blue lagoon
As frail as maidenhair,
Shall dance and sing before your eyes
Amongst the blossoms there.
While on a stem a beetle smiles
Beneath the myrtle tree,
As pixie folk in hats of silk
Sit where your eyes can't see.

Down by the wilderness of sand
Awash with cockleshells,
I'll tell you tales of pirate men
Who sail on caravels, -
While mermaids with unblinking eyes
Swim all the seven seas,
Two cuckoos with a turtle dove
Sing low to honeybees.

Wee leprechauns are everywhere
Within the clover dell,
In velvet suits with silver braid
with flowers in each lapel.
They dwell where rainbows meet the land,
Where rain falls like a mist,
As gentle as a baby's cheek
Caressed and softly kissed.

I see your eyes close on a sigh,
It's time for bed, I know,
Tomorrow I shall tell you where
The Elf King had to go.
For now I'll close my book of rhyme
Without another peep -
And hope you dream a symphony
Within your hours of sleep .....Sh!

Hush

Hush little baby, I'm looking at you,
deep into your eyes of soft peacock blue -
ten fingers and toes that don't have a care
and hair that's not straight nor curly, but fair.

Hush little Baby, I'll tell you no lies;
you're my shining star in soft velvet skies
with sweetness of honey, kindness and grace;
you will bring sunshine to many a face.

Hush little Baby, I'll tell you some tales
of kittens and mice that live in the vales
where fairies and elves cast magical spells -
in the far wood where the unicorn dwells.

Hush little Baby, now hush go to sleep -
tonight no more tales, not even a peep;
here is the sandman to gather your sighs
with magical dust to cover your eyes.

Acorns

Fragile little fairy folk,
tossing acorns in the air
'fore the winter wraps her cloak
'cross the autumn with despair.

Elfin poised with gentle grace,
acorns wreathed upon her brow,
with a tireless, dancing pace
harvesting the oaks right now.

Deer with young turn up to dine
and with squirrels join the queue,
'round the roots that so entwine,
Nature's harvest, they pursue.

Dormouse not to be out-shone,
'neath the boughs of oak she'll creep,
then with fairies one by one,
with their acorns slumber deep.

Ambrosias (The Spell-Keeper)

Beyond the path by yonder wood,
Yet further past the gorse-filled ridge
A hovel in a myrtle tree
Stands bowed beside the witchty bridge.

There's neither name above the door,
Nor is there posted sign to guide –
As creeper vines caress your face,
With wanderings and silent stride.

Ambrosias, for centuries
Has ruled the witches of the land
And warlocks too, whose terrors strike,
By devious means and sleight of hand.

He's dressed in black from head to foot
With pince-nez perched before his eyes,
His legendary name strikes fear
For one foul curse can paralyse.

In ledgers older than himself
Enchantments logged with quills of swan,
While witches eager for his charms
Wait with impatience, one by one.

His faithful owl Ptolemy,
Sits quietly with eyes agape,
Until Ambrosias needs mice,
Or spiders of most any shape.

Or pythons yet with skins intact,
Zig-zagging through the forest aisle,
Along with beetles, black as coal
Creeping beneath the beechwood-pile.

Dried eye of bat and viper's bile
Ambrosias, his mortar fills,
His pestle grinding through the night
The powdered bulbs of daffodils.

His cauldron boils with curdled blood
And has a thousand years or more,
Stewed long beside the witchty bridge
Where bluebells bloom with hellebore.

His daily sips of potent brew
Concocted from his gruesome store,
Sustain and thus enable him
At last, to live! Forevermore.

Fingers and Toes

Tiny fingers, tiny toes,
Smiles to thaw the deepest snows,
Scent of rose and sugared spice,
Honey sweet and all things nice.
Soft as early morning mist,
Cheeks aglow and sunshine-kissed,
Seeking warmth I strive to hold -
Hands within melt from the cold,
Fingers twined as warm as toast
That which takes my humour most,
Eyes awake are pigeon-blue
Telling me dreams do come true.

All of paradise lies here
In my arms, not yet a year.

Belle

At twilight when the wild things wake
around my weary feet
when owls are drifting off to hunt
and all the earth smells sweet,
I walk beyond the sycamores
where shadows meet starlight,
to wonder what at close of day
it is that shines so bright.

A robin with his feathers fluffed
is looking satisfied
as crickets sit about his feet
with spiders alongside
and sat aloft on robin's back
a fairy singing low,
with bells adorning feet and hands
on limbs as white as snow.

I hear the robin call her Belle
then puff his scarlet chest,
prompting the crickets now to sing
with vim and renewed zest,
while beetles dance with ladybirds,
their jeweled wings polished well
with spots of green or black as ink,
in this light who can tell.

Her bells ring out a symphony
within my garden walls,
while I eavesdrop this charming scene
where tender starlight falls.
The air is softly magical
for who has gazed before
upon this sight before my eyes
I silently encore.

Jessica Bonnet

The Queen's coming to tea today
At quarter past the four,
And so's my dolly Annabelle
With George the dinosaur,
Along with Ted and Susie mouse,
Who promises to make
Some cookies made with choc'late chips,
A milkshake and a cake.

The Queen's coming to tea today,
I've not told Mummy yet,
Because she'll get her nervy twitch
And worry with a fret -
Should there be dust around the floor,
Or cobwebs here and there,
Or cushions that may need a plump
On Daddy's comfy chair.

The Queen's coming to tea today,
It's time to dress-up nice,
In party frock and Granma's hat
That smells of musty spice!
With Mummy's lipstick on my face
I'll hold my Teddy's paw,
While George the dinosaur pours tea
As I open the door.

The Queen's coming to tea today ...

Lullaby Faerie

Lullaby faerie from lullaby town,
Wears pretty blue lace with bows on her gown,
With coppery curls and gossamer wings -
Aflutter mid-air, like all flying things.

She enters my room when I'm half asleep,
As quiet as a mouse she takes a wee peep
And if I'm awake she kisses my nose -
With delicate touch, right down to my toes.

Sweet lullaby faerie sing a refrain,
Of kittens in hats or huff–a–puff train,
Or bunnie's pale eyes in Watership Down -
Before you go home to lullaby town.

Maggie Phee

I stumbled 'pon a witch last night,
Her name was Maggie Phee -
In cloak and gown to match her eyes
As black as black can be,
But somethin' 'bout her witchy face
Was gentler than you'd think,
For in those eyes I saw her soul
Had kindness on the brink.

She told me 'bout a curse one day
When spells went awf'ly wrong,
Instead of chanting, 'eyes of bat,'
She'd sung a nurs'ry song!
'Twas then the wizard banished her
To live her life alone -
Along with Maximus her cat,
Into the vast unknown!

She travelled for a thousand years,
With nought to reason why -
On broomsticks ever breaking down
Across the midnight sky,
And so it is whene'er you hear
A lullaby sung low -
'Tis Maggie chanting nurs'ry rhymes,
She learnt so long ago!

Priscilla Caterpillar

Priscilla yawned a perfect yawn
And winked a perfect wink,
As day was overtaking dawn
From night as black as ink.
She stretched her caterpillar feet
Deciding what to do
When suddenly a girl so neat,
Mumbled, 'how do you do.'

'Well I declare,' Priscilla cried
And 'who my dear goes there?'
'Don't stand there mumbling under breath
And don't look in despair.'
You might deduce from those last words
Priscilla took offence,
At interruptions to her day
From this girl looking tense.

The toadstool where Priscilla sat
Was high enough to see
The girl who in a pleasing dress
Was just about to flee.
'Now come here girl,' Priscilla said
And drawing near she stooped,
Sighing, she gazed upon the girl
With shoulders round and drooped

Diplomacy, Priscilla lacked
So asked the girl outright,
Just what it was she mumbled for
And pray what was her plight.
The girl, barefoot and trembling now
Was blinded by the stars,
When walking through enchanted woods
And couldn't find grandma's.

Priscilla thought a little thought
And wriggled her sweet nose,
She said it was about her time
To pupate and transpose.
The young girl watched transfixed with glare
As promptly without fail,
Priscilla changed before her eyes
Into a swallowtail.

'And now dear girl I'll take you home
So climb upon my wings
And we shall fly to grandmama's
Where apple blossom sings.'
Over the patterned vales they flew,
Beneath a clear blue sky
And there just by the wooden bridge
Descended with a sigh.

There is a magic place I've heard
You'll see a swallowtail,
Where if you sit without a word
Her wings she will unfurl.
And there you'll see a little smudge
Just where the small girl sat,
To journey home to grandmama,
In far off Astolat.

Why?

There's someone who'll know
And tell when I'm four,
Why sand ripples white upon the seashore
And why a kiss means I'm loved beyond doubt,
By Mommy and Pa and puppy's warm snout.

There's someone who'll know
And tell when I'm six,
Whatever it means by, 'Oh fiddlesticks'
And why lullabies when sung by my bed,
Make faerie-folk dance round my sleepy head.

There's someone who'll know
And tell when I'm eight,
Why dragons breathe fire and stairs escalate,
Then why my ice-cream should melt in my hand
And why when it rains do cows never stand.

There's someone who'll know
And tell when I'm twelve,
If spaceships to Mars will search and then delve -
Into the unknown where myst'ries are deep
Beyond where the Moon is trying to sleep.

There's someone who'll know
And tell when I'm old,
Why raindrops that fall can never be sold,
And why I can't catch the wind when I run,
With arms open wide,

Please tell me someone.

Snow Faerie

You fall and flutter with delight,
Leaving prints from dainty feet,
Freezing cold your wintry bite
'Pon the trees and city streets.

Dressed in silv'ry robe-like gowns,
Only winter dares to wear -
Through the dales and through the towns
Painting scapes with ne'er a care.

Plummeting to earth with grace,
Lithe and sprightly on my lawn,
Where the willows slow embrace
Flakes of snow as night meets dawn.

Of the faeries that I know,
You're the fairest of them all,
White with beauty, faerie snow
Waiting now for winter's call!

A Princess for Spring

Come see the Princess of the land,
Behold her tiny outstretched hand,
For she's arrived along with spring,
This baby of the Queen and King.
Such love awaits this fair Princess,
As all who meet her will caress
Her peach-soft skin and hair spunned gold
Such beauty never seen, I'm told.

She's born with love and in good time,
When all is budding and sublime,
As primroses with daffodils
Sit high and low upon the hills
While Mr Robin sings with zest,
A puffing out his scarlet vest
To all who come within his sight,
From dawn's first crow to soft twilight.

And as she lay, this babe not one,
In blankets soft of wool homespun,
Each fairy of the land will fly
To rock the cradle by and by,
On wings of gold and silver lace
They'll sprinkle stardust to embrace
A charm, erasing all her fears
Whereby, she'll only shed kind tears.

These nymphs will nurse and shelter her,
Against evils that may bestir
And some will whisper lullabies
And should she cry they'll murmur sighs.
With magic they will keep her warm,
Like fledglings in a nest of haulm
Safe from the dragons to be slain
Still roaming yonder on the plain.

Meanwhile the jesters of the court
Frolic with dancing to disport,
While trumpets blare and cuckoos sing
And magpies twitter on the wing.
Such pageantry has not been seen,
Not since the King married the Queen
And when this day of joy is done,
They'll view the setting of the sun.

Twilight (Quartern)

When half the sky is at twilight
And owls that hunt dive to ensnare
As crickets chant and mice recite,
Then I see magic everywhere.

The moon is lonely, drifting high
When half the sky is at twilight
And fairies start to flutter by,
As silver moonbeams shimmer white.

I'm like a child to see this sight
As from the window I look through,
When half the sky is at twilight
And fairy folk come into view.

My garden seems a magic place
As fairies hold the moonbeams tight,
In tiny hands so full of grace
When half the sky is at twilight.

The Faerie Wedding

The wedding day was here at last, all preparations made,
With elves and gnomes the list was fast assembling in the glade.
The faerie King would take the hand of Princess Bonny Claire,
And all the nymphs in faerie land would join this wedding fair.

The king was seated on his throne, to hear the wedding march,
He sat serene but all alone beneath the perfumed arch.
When suddenly he heard the throng and laughter filled the air,
As swans carried his bride along, through swathes of maidenhair.

Green leprechauns with beards long and goblins looking sprite,
In suits of red they sang a song, much to the King's delight.
Two brownies on a pea-green float had faerie dust to throw,
While Master Magpie in frock-coat flew ribbons white as snow.

The cockroaches, along with bats wore breeches of fine suede,
O'er fancy shoes beneath white spats to join in the parade.
Pixies in hats of columbine, with matching tunic dress -
And imps with leaves to soft entwine, the hair of the Princess.

White mice were pulling acorn shells for baby frogs to ride,
While snails were urged to carry spells and toadstools for the bride.
A butterfly, wings delicate guided the Princess fair,
Whose gown, bejewelled and intricate was sewn by Mistress Hare.

A turtle dove recited vows for bride and groom to make.
And all the faeries sighing soughs had brought along a cake.
While harebells rang and petals strewn upon this magic scene,
Even the stars and sequinned moon bowed to the King and Queen.

The Jays and The Faerie Queen

The woodland boasts fine-looking birds but none quite like the jay,
Whose wingtips of a turquoise blue one sees from far away.
Their tails are black as dark as coal in contrast with the white,
That sits pink flecked upon the crown, soft gleaming in the light.

Pure whiteness on the underside will blaze before your eyes,
In autumn when the acorns fall beneath grey speckled skies.
A few are shy and out of sight but only yesterday -
I saw between two giant ferns a group of jays at play.

I stood as quiet as a mouse beside a cypress fir,
Without a murmur from my voice nor hand nor foot astir.
'Twas then I saw the Faerie Queen with bells around her feet
And soft entwined about her hair a wreath of marguerite.

While magic floated on the breeze before the twilight moon,
Across the woodland glade she stepped with scented pines bestrewn.
She danced around the woodland jays whose mantles were ashine,
With pride and wonder and content between the ranks of pine.

I could not bring the wonder home I saw amongst the trees,
Beneath the woodland's canopy with perfume on the breeze.
Beyond these words I say to you I saw such lovely things,
Clear let me keep the sight of jays with turquoise on their wings.

Goblin's Pool

Beneath the bridge there's water
They call the goblin's pool,
Where willows bend to whisper
To keep all crystal cool,
For 'neath the polished rainbow,
There is a charming sight,
Just as the day surrenders
To shadows at twilight.

Beneath the bridge there's laughter
While stars twinkle above,
Upon the gurgling water
With chuckles from a dove,
For bathing in the moonlight
Amongst the maidenhair,
Are fairy folk and pixies,
Midst every colour there.

Beyond the bridge there're dragons
Guarding the wicked witch,
Who'll cast a spell of evil
From cauldrons black as pitch,
You'll see her fly at midnight
In robes as dark as sky,
Then the fairies never laugh,
For she will terrify!

Here by the bridge at twilight,
Below the castle's glare,
The fairy folk are playing
With bubbles in the air,
Their wings almost transparent
Are kissing in the breeze
And all around there's perfume
From blossoms on the trees.

Beneath the bridge there's water
They call the goblin's pool,
Where 'neath moonshine the fairies
Gather in palest tulle,
I shan't forget I've seen them
As I bid each farewell,
And turn towards the mountain,
Nor will I ever tell ....

Colours I know

I know the sky is pale sometimes,
With rain it's pearly grey
But when it's white as silver mist
I know snow's on its way.

It's red sometimes like my balloon
Or pinker than my shoes,
But most of all *I know* it's best
When full of peacock blues.

At night the dark blots out the day,
Yet doesn't frighten me
For when I wake *I know* it's there
With colours I can see.

The Flower Faerie

The flower faerie slowly wakes
when spring is almost due,
she's slept the winter months tight-curled
beneath the tall bamboo,
where moss has kept her warm throughout
each day of rain and cold,
as with the dormouse safe she lay
'neath mists of pearl and gold.

But as the periwinkle sky
grows warmer by the day,
'tis when the flower faerie stirs
to scent each bloom's bouquet,
so primrose and forget-me-not
smell lovelier by far,
as sumptuously she nurtures all
amongst her repertoire.

Each petal cup she breaths upon
as dragonflies drift by,
'twixt hellebore and marigolds,
and daffodils, knee high.
From autumn's flame to summer's green -
each petal's slow unfurled,
for every flower now smells divine
in her part of the world.

On wings of gossamer and lace,
without a sound nor sigh,
she'll hover on the slightest breeze,
beneath the palest sky.
Yet when the gardens go to sleep
as winter starts to chill,
again she'll sleep tight-curled and warm
beside the dormouse still.

The Magic Forest

Oh, what magic in this forest
Where moonbeams gently fall,
Where jade blue pines are numinous
When night time comes to call.
And stars silver and glistening
At play with leaf and fern,
While snowy owls drift on the breeze
With anything nocturne.

I hear the crickets plaintive tune
As bats skim overhead,
While noises from the undergrowth
Are filling me with dread.
Between the trembling hanging vines,
I sense I'm almost there,
I've crept here once or twice before -
In wonderment to stare.

For here I see the fairy mound
Deep in the sheltered grove,
I'm blinded by the mystic light,
Where all shines misty mauve.
These nymphs I spy in petal gowns
With arms like buttermilk,
Begin to dance and murmur songs
In voices soft as silk.

At night when everything is still
These fairies are not shy,
They dance when dark and rarely sleep,
While days go softly by.
And high above the naked moon,
The stars look down with charm
And should you see these laughing nymphs,
Then you'll be free from harm.

Mary

If you chance upon a toadstool
When the moon is riding high,
O'er a softly singing whirlpool
'Neath a purple velvet sky,
You may catch sight of a faerie
Just beyond the dragon's lair,
Where the verdant shades may vary
Midst the orchids, ever rare.

She's cross-legged upon her toadstool
As a lark swoops on the wing,
Watching voles with crickets tomfool
Round the little faerie ring,
While the blackbirds one and twenty
Sing of puddings and a pie,
There are ladybirds aplenty,
And a moth who's rather shy.

If you chance upon this faerie
She'll be 'neath the moonbeams glow,
And I know her name is Mary,
For the dormouse told me so.
She's the keeper of the moonshine,
Making sure it glistens bright
For the lovers who will entwine,
While the nightingale's in flight.

Cornflower Faeries

At twilight when I see the owls
drift overhead to dart and skim,
when all the sky is pink and low
and all my garden's looking dim,
    the cornflowers shake and tremble sweet
    as faeries flirt on slippered feet.

Upon each flower head they play
to sway with ev'ry little breeze,
as crickets chant their evening call
and spider hangs from his trapeze,
  while caterpillars wave their arms
  enchanted by these faerie charms.

On every stem and every leaf
they flit in gowns of palest blue
and every bud not yet in bloom
they sprinkle with the bluest hue,
  from pale to dark with sapphire tinge
  they frolic at my gardens fringe.

I can't imagine it's not true
that in this flower-bed I see,
a dozen faeries on the wing
and they're all looking up at me,
  as crickets cease their evening call
  until I'm gone, before nightfall.

The Mermaid and The Dragons

She sat upon the sandstone rock
To comb each curl and tangled lock,
Beneath the moon now blotting out the day.
Her comb of silver was now old
But teased her tresses flecked with gold,
A treasure she had found along the bay.

Deep from the oceans tidal lure
She slow emerged glist'ning and pure
Upon the smooth and sloping creamy sand,
Where pelicans had said, 'hello,'
Upon the beach as white as snow
And in return she'd waved her soft, pale hand.

A thousand miles she'd swum today
Along with dolphins and a ray,
So happy to escort their mermaid queen.
They knew she had to get here fast,
Through oceans brooding, wide and vast,
To rendezvous with dragons, turquoise green.

She'd travelled from a far off land
With neither kin, friend nor husband,
Through fear she had been banished from her throne.
For once she'd been a mighty queen
And ruled the seas beyond Lazbene,
Until ousted by monsters unbeknown.

Alas, that's how it came to be,
She lost her realm and monarchy
And now seeks comfort where the combers roll,
Where gentle dragon's fiery breath
Means hearing bird song 'stead of death
Where she can bathe her lonely voiceless soul.

Afraid, she sat upon a rock,
When suddenly and with a shock,
She spied a dragon with a welcome smile
And as she sat there by the sea,
Upon the beach of ivory
She told the dragons of her sad exile.

Enchanted, were the dragons green
To gaze upon the mermaid queen,
Such beauty never loomed before their eyes.
They said they'd guard her with a charm
And keep her safe and free from harm,
Upon their land beneath the storm-free skies.

The dragons reigned for countless years,
Protecting all from buccaneers
With magic conjured up in their wisdom.
The mermaid queen was tired and sad,
She needed hope she'd never had
So asked that she may stay in their kingdom.

And now when days are cool and bare,
You'll catch a glimpse of gold flecked hair,
In seas of kissing waves that gently play.
Where swims a mermaid with delight
Beneath horizons crystal white
Whilst dragons, turquoise green watch from the bay.

Puddle Faerie

I know a faerie small and light,
Who slumbers curled within the rose,
As raindrops kiss her pretty head
And tickle each of all her toes.
She never likes to show herself
Until the rain begins to fall,
But when it does she'll wake from sleep
To stand beside the rushes tall.

With eyes ashine for love of rain
And smiles on her expressive face,
She sings for joy before she fluffs
Her wings of silver-spun fine lace,
Yet doesn't waste a single chance
To dip her toes with great content,
And fly from hanging vine and rose,
To smell the heady, rain kissed scent.

Before the sun can dry the land
She calls all life that needs to drink,
Each cricket, frog and butterfly -
Each crane in grey with crown of pink.
She shakes her wand and gown of silk
And joins the birds to drink the rain,
And with a splish and splash and splosh
Circles to swoop and drink again.

She always seems to have wet feet,
When all the earth smells damp and sweet.

Silver Faerie

She sits poised in the crystal air
beneath the silver clouds on high,
her wings of lace are now at rest
as night descends and crickets sigh.

I see her from the shadows near
a silver stream where swans embrace
the coming of the silver night,
where heaven smiles at her sweet grace.

A moonbeam plays upon her lips
As lovely as tomorrow's sun,
and as she smiles I see her gown
of gossamer with silver spun.

Now as I peer into the night
below the stars in silver strands,
I catch a whisper of her hair
and see the flutter of her hands.

There's not a sound for nothing moves
save for the little silver stream,
is this some magic that I feel,
or has my heart succumbed to dream?

The Proposal

She sat for weeks with King and Queen,
This princess of the land,
As gifts of gold and rare baleen
Were offered for her hand,
Enticing her with silks and fur
And kittens with the softest purr,
Enticing her
Enticing her
With diamonds, frankincense and myrrh.

With eyes downcast she shook her head
And scowled her weary brow,
As suitors, mostly thoroughbred
Just didn't suit somehow,
With promises of moon and stars
And Russian trips to meet the tsars,
With promises
With promises
Of cakes and tea from samovars.

So in despair she sat to weep,
With hopes of real love soon
And like a child she fell asleep
Beneath the shining moon,
That beckoned her with dreams of love
From constellations high above,
That beckoned her
That beckoned her
With cupid's hand in velvet glove.

She woke into a face she knew
From riding through the dene,
A handsome man of some virtue
Whose skill lay in things treen.
With hand on heart his love he vowed

And kissing her he gently bowed,
With hand on heart
With hand on heart
The carpenter was wholly proud.

And so it came to pass next day
With blessings from the king,
The princess kissed her fiancé
Beneath the bells ringing.
Such happiness is crisp and sweet
When dreams are met with one heartbeat,
Such happiness
Such happiness
When love is pure and so complete.

And all the birds and all the bees
And cats that wail and waul,
Looked down from all the laughing trees,
At all the wherewithal.
And fairy queen danced all the night,
As did the stars so pearly white
And fairy queen
And fairy queen
Danced 'neath the moon 'til dawn's first light.

Miss Twizzy's Midnight Visitor

'Twas one past the midnight when Miss Twizzy Mouse
was woken by something elsewhere in the house,
she'd heard a commotion, a sound from the roof,
a strange stomping sound like a soft reindeer hoof.

'Please let it be Santa' she heard herself cry,
with tears of excitement she couldn't deny,
before she could count past two, three and four
she felt Santa placing a gift in each paw.

A rosy-red apple with nibbles of cheese,
apricot nougat and warm dungarees -
to wear when escaping the old portly cat
and to keep ears cosy, a red velvet hat.

'Twas two past the midnight, now Santa was gone
as snow started falling and everywhere shone,
while all round the house there was nothing astir,
except for the rumble of portly cat's purr....Shhhhh!

A Bit of Nonsense ....

Nonsense

In the Heb-ri-des
Where the summers freeze
And the monkey's nose turns blue,
There's a pink giraffe
With a phonograph
And the mice sing nicky nacky noo.
While the trees go bang,
All the cats rhyme slang
And you only understand a few,
Then it's hard to say
Why the spiders' neigh
And the mice sing nicky nacky noo,
When the hippos' cry
In the old pigsty
Tiger tickles kangaroo,
So it's chin chan chonk
From the honky-tonk,
While the mice sing nicky nacky noo.

Box Of Frogs

When I'm eating lunch at tea-time
In the garden where it's warm
Disenchantment overwhelms me
As two bees attract a swarm;
Have you noticed how Mick Jagger
Likes brown sugar all the time
When it's half past four and twenty
And the poet can't spell rhyme;
Let the swallows eat the roses
With their beaks of molten gold
Did I tell you how I'm feeling
Like a box of frogs and cold.

When Tony Bennett Picks A Plum

When Tony Bennett picks a plum
From the tree of life,
So Frank Sinatra sings of sharks
Annoying Mack the knife,
Then asking me where are the clowns,
By the great Sondheim,
Then I won't write of poetry that doesn't have a rhyme.

And when Dean Martin croons of things
That make me want to cry,
Then with a whisky in his hand
He'll hum, I don't know why,
But when no mountain's high enough
For Marvin Gaye to climb,
Then I won't write of poetry that doesn't have a rhyme.

When Sade says your love is king,
Just singing by your side,
Or when The Beatles ask for help
Wanting tickets to ride,
When Black Eyed Peas meet me halfway
And Pink Floyd echoes time,
Then I won't write of poetry that doesn't have a rhyme.

If Streisand sings the way we were,
Or if you go away,
In the park on Sunday
When funny girl won't play,
Or when I hear of Bette Midler
Sing swinging from a vine,
Then I won't write of poetry that doesn't have a rhyme.

When dying in your arms tonight
Means more than just a song,
As there's no more tomorrow
Because our life's been long,
When eulogies have all been said,
In spring or summertime,
Then I won't write of poetry that doesn't have a rhyme.

Got To Be In Rhyme

I'll sing a verse of poetry,
I'll rap to you one time,
Whatever your request may be
'Tis got to be in rhyme!

I'll sing a hymn from songs of praise,
I'll scat the blues for you,
Of foggy days in London town
Where lovers rendezvous.

I'll yodel, yodel-hey-hee,
I'll hum a lullaby,
For you to rock to dreamy-byes
In cradles swingin' high.

I'll croon of adolescent love,
I'll purr a soft refrain,
Of kisses sweet as honeycomb
Or dancin' in the rain.

I'll carol-sing of Bethlehem,
I'll jingle Rudolph's bell,
Albeit....... I'm out of tune -
But hey there, what the hell!!!

Arthur Or Martha

When I can't see rhyme nor reason
For a day that's full of chores
When I could be writing verses
'Bout archaic dinosaurs,
Or a poem for the mermaids
Or a poem for the bee
Or a poem for the dreamers
Pensive 'neath the willow tree.

When I don't know where I'm going
Or I'm coming here and there
When adventures seem a plenty
For my quill to kindly share,
With a poem for the fairies
With a poem for the elf
With a poem for the teddies
Smiling on the nursery shelf.

When I can't tell if I'm Arthur
Or a Martha in disguise
When the summer turns to winter
And there's torment in the skies,
I can write 'til moonlight shadows
I can write 'til break of day
I can write 'til summer's warming
Shining on the buds of May.

When I'm feeling slightly dally
With a shilly shally smile
When the muse within starts waning
To lay dormant for a while,
There's no hope of inspiration
There's no hope of pantomime
There's no hope of adulation
For my poetry of rhyme.

I Think I'm Sick

I have a cold. I think I'm sick.
I cough and sneeze. I feel chronic.
I struggle now to take a breath,
I think I must be close to death!

I stay in bed. I cannot sleep.
I try to read. I count the sheep.
I toss and turn, then cough some more,
Is someone knocking my front door?

I miss the dogs, I miss the fun.
I need to walk. I want to run.
I need a glass of wine at least
Or better still, wine with a feast.

I sigh a sigh. I feel worn out.
I want to cry. I want to shout.
It's been a week since I felt well,
Now someone's ringing my doorbell.

My throat is sore. My hair's a mess
I look like hell, I must confess.
My voice is hoarse, it hurts me too,
Methinks I may have caught man-flu!

.............and *still* the doorbell's ringing

When Young (Clerihew)

When young I looked like Doris Day
The Queen of Hollywood cliche
I danced and sang with all her zest
But now I look more like Mae West!!!

Must Be Champagne

I love a glass of bubbly
When it's time to spread good cheer,
When celebrations call for
More expensive taste than beer.
Should friends be getting married
When I'm dressed up to the nines,
I'll raise a glass of bubbly
From the best of Champagne vines.
I don't prefer martinis
Shaken sweet or even dry,
Or vermouth soured with lemon
Seems to make me want to cry!
A whisky soda's bitter -
And tequila slammers too,
Along with schnapps and cointreau,
Barley wine and Pop's home brew.
I sipped a Marguarita
At a party yesterday,
Well, maybe more than one -
Because the room began to sway.
Bacardi makes me whoozy,
Mixed with a lemonade
And cocktails leave me speechless
With a head like a grenade.
I've tried Pina Coladas
And the odd lager with lime,
But then can't write a poem -
'Cos the words don't seem to rhyme.
And so it MUST be Champagne
From the grapes of Chardonnay,
At Christmas time and New Year,
More especially my birthday.
So today and all tomorrows
(Or least 'til my memoirs,)
I'll sip a glass of bubbly Feeling like I'm drinking stars.

I Won't sing

Some people say, come sing along,
Join in the karaoke
Alas, my voice is out of synch,
Out of tune 'n' croaky.
I'd love to purr a love song
Or croon a lullaby
Or swing the blues like Ella,
Rod Stewart or Macfly.

The stage is full of wannabe's,
From teens to aging men,
Some are ghastly, some are worse
While some sound like Big Ben.
Some just want to emulate
Chuck Berry's Ding a Ling
Me, I'll boogie woogie...... but
Don't ask 'cos, I won't sing.

The Three of Us

The image in the mirror'd glass
Is Granmama, not me,
Yet as I touch her wrinkled brow
I'm not sure who I see!

It seems not awf'ly long ago
T'was Mother gazing back,
That's when I dyed my hair again
From grey to almost black.

There's times I think a nip an' tuck
Would cure this malady,
Then *only* could the three of us
Reflect in harmony!!!!

Do I Want?

Now do I want a man who's young,
Who wears white tees with jeans low-slung,
Who's showing off his bronzed six pack
Yet can't spell aphrodisiac?
Of course I like a nice physique -
With muscles honed, sinewy sleek,
But I desire *not* to compete
With working to a rapper's beat.

He'll play football, or maybe darts
While I visit the Tate's fine arts
And sex will be another sport,
(I s'pect I'll need a knee support!!)
But worse than that, he'll come home drunk,
And smelling like a randy skunk,
He'll wake me from my beauty sleep
Where I'll be counting endless sheep!

I'll have to keep in tip-top shape
And hoist my boobs with sellotape,
Keep my bikini line at bay
And stop my hair from going grey.
He'll play his music overloud
While boasting that he's well endowed,
When all I want's a quiet stroll,
Or maybe cook a casserole!

He'll pub and club 'til after hours
And then apologise with flowers,
His car will be his pride and joy,
I'll just become *another* toy.
I've done all this, so long ago
But settle now for sweet cocoa,
And Dan the man with balding pate,
Who carries maybe too much weight.

So do I want a man who's young,
Who's highly fit and highly strung
While friends say, "cor, look at his pecs,"
Course I will.......*now where's my specs?*

A Light Read

Late afternoon with Mills and Boon,
She cries a thousand tears,
For heroines in crinolines
In love with buccaneers.

Before twilight, a handsome knight
Will step right off the page,
While she sips tea, enthralled you see
With stories to assuage.

With hearts afire and grand desire
And scandals in the sun,
Each page she'll turn with great concern
For lovers on the run.

With tear filled eyes it signifies,
The final chapters read,
Late afternoon with Mills and Boon,
Who said romance was dead!!

The Hangover

I lie in bed at break of day
With hopes the sun is on its way,
Just thinking of the day ahead
Beneath my quilted rose bedspread.
Shall my today be mirth or joy,
Sweet ecstasy or frightful ploy
And do I want to face this dawn,
I'll stretch and have another yawn!

Meanwhile, I hear the clock's alarm
As I recall Omar Khayyam,
Perhaps I'll read another verse
Before I start to feel much worse.
I'd like to stay in bed today,
Why did I drink the Beaujolais?
If only there was someone who
Could make a cup of strongTyphoo!

Damn! No good, I must arise
To wash my face and moisturise,
A soft boiled egg or Shredded Wheat?
I'm not too steady on my feet,
I think I'll just pop back to bed,
My eyes are looking blurry, red,
I'm really not a pretty sight,
My brain and mouth will not unite.

Now back in bed I snuggle down,
My face scowls madly in a frown
For something niggles in my mind,
My God! How could I be so blind?
I sit bolt upright there to see
My dogs, young Ted and sweet Dolly,
Who must be walked and duly fed,
Oh!!! I'm such a knucklehead!!!

Men of a Certain Age

Why do men of a certain age
Lust for a Playboy scorcher
Or bimbos' with enormous boobs
(Who've gone through pain and torture)
These men who've seen the best of days
Want young girls to desire -
With teeth perfectly straight and white
And skin so taut in jeans so tight
With bums as hard as Bakelite
To set old flames afire

Why do men of a certain age
Lust for a Playboy beauty
Or Dollys' tanned with bleach blonde hair
Who shake and roll their booty
These men who've seen the best of days
Want to recapture youth -
By having sexy fuelled affairs
With corset covered derrieres
Behind closed doors and portieres
They're crazy ...... that's the truth!!!

Jude

There was once a strip-teaser called Jude
Who ate lots of fatty junk food
She became over-weight
As she constantly ate
So her contract was never renewed

Beyond Hamelin

The pied piper of Hamelin Town
Is not the man you knew,
No longer is he thin and tall
With eyes the sharpest blue.
He's now a hundred years or more,
With still no kith nor kin
But whisk'ry now about the face
To hide his swarthy skin.
He's rather stout with balding pate
Yet still wears quaint attire,
His buckled shoes and yellow coat
Many would still admire.

He's poor, just as he's always been,
The council never paid
A thousand guilders long ago,
When townsfolk were afraid.
When rats of every size and hue
Came tumbling out of doors,
From street to street and step to step
They followed by the scores
The piper as he rid the plague
And drowned until, 'no more,'
Except for one called Julius,
Who swam to the far shore.

But when the piper asked the Mayor
For payment he was shocked,
To hear such words as, 'go from here
Before I have you stocked.'
The piper cried, 'don't do this sir,
Again my pipe I'll play
And all the children of this town
Shall follow me this day.'
And that is how he came to be

Beyond the mountainside,
Where unicorns have silver wings
And no-one's ever cried.

The one surviving rat followed
The children as they ran,
Towards the mountain o'er the hills,
Which was the piper's plan
And there a portal opened wide
Enough to let them pass -
But shut as fast for evermore
On Hamelin's upper-class .
Alas, alas there was but naught
That anyone could do,
The piper with his magic pipe
Had led the children through.

And so in all these hundred years
The piper and the rat,
Have lived beyond the portal where
Together they've grown fat,
Alongside all the boys and girls
Who'd willingly followed
The pipe with magic in its notes
With shouting, over-awed,
When little feet in wooden shoes
Had clattered at a run,
And little hands had clapped with glee,
Beneath the mid-day sun.

'Twas when the mountainside shut fast
The piper sat a while,
To lay his pipe upon the grass
Of sweetest camomile
Then turned to Julius the rat
And with a smile he said,
'Here my dear friend is where I'll stay,
Until I'm truly dead.'

But now that he is very old
There's neither sound nor trace,
Of any magic or a pipe,
Playing, to soft embrace!

Sudoku

The numbers in my head are there,
To place in rows in ev'ry square
Of this Sudoku game today,
That's driving me ev'ry which way.
My head is spinning with a nine
That simply will not fit a line.

I tried this morning before lunch,
Because I had a certain hunch
That if I moved the five and three,
I'd gain a sure-fire victory.
Alas, the nine popped up again,
To make my head split with the pain.

My tea-time passed, now dinner too,
But still I've neither hint nor clue,
My pencil's blunt trying to find
The answer, but I am resigned
To failure one too many times,
So I'll continue penning rhymes.

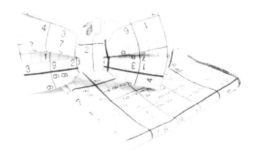

The Banshees Wail

'Twas just a day or two before
The eve of Halloween,
When witches from another land
Were eager to be seen,
To make their mischief where they can
And even in between -
Wherever they can bring about
Spells, pitilessly mean.

Between the hours of two and three,
Or was it three and four
On such a day as I recall
I trembled to the core,
For out of greyness in the sky
There came a mighty roar,
That splintered every pane of glass
And rattled every door.

The sky grew dark as if the night
Had suddenly besmeared
The afternoon with daubs of ink,
Astonishingly weird,
As with a moaning and a howl
The banshees wail appeared,
With eyes aflame and gaping mouth
That positively sneered.

The wail had no embodiment,
Well, none that I could see
And wondered if her wailing meant
My own deaths prophesy -
Or were the witches playing tricks
With spells as dark as night,
Or was I dreaming nightmares long
Before the morning light?

Pumpkin Jack

Now Pumpkin Jack sleeps all the year
Except at Halloween,
That's when he wakes at Summer's End
To don his coat of green.

With silver buttons on red braid
And waistcoat of brocade,
All tailored many years ago
But now starting to fade.

In just one night he tours the land
To drive demons away,
As at each house he lights lanterns,
To keep spirits at bay.

Along with all the ghoulie ghosts
And spiders on witch hats,
Tall skeletons that come to life
And silly tiresome bats.

But once he's lit his lantern head
He knows what he must do,
To help the children 'trick or treat'
Before the night is through.

So hand in hand they follow him
To ward off harmful spooks,
But hide their faces behind masks
When meeting gobbl'ygooks.

Alas, Jack's mean side takes over
And Devil's promise made,
To keep him from the gates of Hell
He must make you afraid.

So when children in fun costumes
Are laden down with treats,
Jack will appear to scare them all
And chase them round the streets.

Thus, should you see old Pumpkin Jack
This coming night of fun,
Be very wary and discreet
And be ready to run!!!

Camberwell

When it's almost two to thirty
On a winters day in June
Ninety four moo cows are dancin'
To a fiddle play'd in tune,
And a gopher in a swimsuit
Shades of honey-coloured blue
Thinks it's nearly ten to forty
Time to start the barbecue;
Now it's raining, pitter patter
And the barbecue won't light
And the cows have stopped their mooing
And the gopher's taken fright,
By the pitter patter raindrops
falling louder than a bell
when it's twenty now to fifty
on the green at Camberwell !

Red Riding Hood

Red Riding Hood, full understood
  The stories from her youth,
Told by mama, in her boudoir
  Of wolves that were uncouth.

Her path well-worn, one early morn
  Into the forest led,
Where vines entwined, were so inclined
  To cause fear where she tread.

Then in disguise, to her surprise
  A wolf made himself known
And said a smile, would help exile
  The spell from an old crone.

Just one small kiss, won't go amiss
  So with much haste and speed,
She kissed his nose, then with repose
  Hoped soon he would be freed.

'Twas then she saw, without a flaw
  Nor yet even a trace
Of wolf to harm, but with a charm
  He looked into her face.

His body bare, he was aware
  Her breaths of mortal sighs,
Enflamed desire, to light his fire
  In his now human eyes.

With gentleness and warm caress
  He kissed her silken lips
And loved her there, in his warm lair
  Just where the hollow dips.

She cried aloud and softly soughed
  And from her tears he sipped,
Then stroked her flesh, in half darkness
  As sun with moon eclipsed.

Red Riding Hood, misunderstood
  The stories from her youth,
Told by mama, in her boudoir
  Of wolves that were uncouth!!!

Sundae Best

New shoes are like an ice-cream treat,
So sensuous and cool,
In every style to suit your feet
From court shoe to a mule.
A ballerina flat in pink,
Sky blue or leopard skin,
Perhaps a heel to make boys wink,
Slipper or moccasin.
Peep-toes look sexy with a heel
While ankle-straps are hip,
To give legs shape and sex-appeal
If made with craftsmanship.
And flip-flops come in every shade
More like a sorbet treat,
With tones of sweetened lemonade,
Vanilla or pale wheat.
Today I'm wearing new red shoes,
While eating strawberry ice,
As tasty as my Jimmy Choos .... -
But less than half the price !!!

Dreamland .....

Before the Sandman

When tucked as snug as any bug cosy in bed at night,
before the sandman reassures with arms holding me tight,
I drift perhaps to dream awhile beneath the silv'ry moon
that winks aloft in velvet skies with stars to guide Neptune.
 Sometimes I see a sailing ship, more often there's a fleet
with golden oars to sweep each wave as drums roll out their beat,
above the creaking of the decks awash from oceans deep,
in rhythm moving steadily yet still not coaxing sleep.
 Or maybe hear a voice calling that speaks a foreign tongue
and on a puff of wind spices to smell from lands far-flung,
as pennons trail above the masts beneath a liquid sky,
while sails of canvas scream at winds around me where I lie.
 Their shadows play upon my walls, for now no sound I hear
As silently their course is steered above the exosphere,
now warm and drowsy, feeling tired I watch the fleet sail west
to navigate horizons new as sleep takes me to rest.

Please Tell Me?

It's such a tiresome thing to do
To lie and watch the whole night through
When frightening nightmares over-run
But soothing comfort there is none
Instead I feel a lingering death
Why can't I hear another's breath
Why can't I bathe my desperate soul
Or ease my aching limbs with oil
Morning and night they are the same
Where is life's vibrancy and flame
I hear songbirds but not their song
I must have done something so wrong
And when the morn brings tears for kin
Please tell me where life will begin

Firelight

On cold and dreary winter nights beside the firelight's glow,
I picture damsels in distress from times of long ago,
At Camelot when knights were bold and Guinevere was Queen,
And all the goings on at court, with jousting in-between.
  Sometimes I see the faerie-folk in gowns of tulle and lace,
Admonishing a leprechaun for playing drums 'n' bass
And singin' ditties over-loud or limericks with mirth -
Of pixies cleverer than me and from a foreign earth.
  Then suddenly between the sparks, a goat in bowler hat
Plays fiddle for a dog that sings a medley in G Flat,
So kittens' sing-a-long for fun with tambourines held high,
While mice in pretty party frocks serve all with pumpkin pie.
  And when the flames start dying down I'm nudged by puppy's snout,
So yawning, climb the wooden stairs .... Because the fires gone out !

The Sandman

I love to see the sandman when at night he comes to call
To sprinkle magic dust around my eyes.
He tells me not to worry on a breath calling for sleep,
As from afar I hear soft lullabies.
  Like a crescent moon his face beams like a million stars,
With eyes darker than bats that dart and skim.
His coat of silk's a shimmer like a brightly-coloured flame,
To drape around his body tall and slim.
  I drift to constellations on the dark side of the sky
Where stars ashine are sparkling crystal-white
And where moon-maids for me alone will sing in their own tongue,
With wishes to behold still shining bright.
  I slumber through my dreams until dawn's light peeps through the sky,
With whisperings to start a brand new day,
Together from night-shadows we shall hear the blackbirds sing
And thoughts of sleep will slowly fade away.

He Dreams

I see my love -
My handsome love
Sleep soundly for a while,
With dreams of far-off places
Slow cruising down the Nile.
In awe of sphinx and pyramids – He speaks a foreign tongue
To scribes with thoughts of wisdom
And lessons for the young.

He sees a tomb -
A Pharoah's tomb
Embalmed so long ago,
With scarabs for protection
'Neath afterlife's tableau.
Of journeys to the underworld – With ivory and gold,
Pale alabaster bottles
And chariots, threefold.

He dreams of Kings -
Of Queens and Kings
And deities of war,
With twenty thousand soldiers
Defending Giza's shore.
With victory for Ramesses - and Gods of moon and sky -
Such dreams he'll not remember,
When asked by you and I!

The Dream Tree

The dream tree sits atop the world
Beneath the sequined moon,
That glistens in the velvet sky
As smooth as a balloon,
Where twinkling stars dance in delight
To cast light on the tree,
Its branches bathing in the glow
So that our dreams may be.

The tree is guarded well, you know
For dreams are treasured gold
With serpents coiled around the trunk
To hiss and scare the bold.
While snowy owls on wings of love
And wood nymphs who enchant,
Try to convey our dreams desired
Asking the tree to grant.

The tree is shaken once a year
Where dreams become stardust,
When fairies of another land
Must cease their wanderlust,
To sort the dreams for happiness
And those to stay tight furled
While all the while the tree of dreams,
Still sits atop the world.

A Touch of Blarney ....

Sean Macardles

Sean Macardles many notions
Seem to set the tongues awag,
Fer 'is notions aren't too clever
And he often likes to brag,
'bout the deeds since long accomplished
In the years since he was born -
In the years since bein' a nipper,
'fore he got so weatherworn.

Now I'll try and tell yer kindly
How yer 'll not mistake 'is look,
In 'is suit of orange velvet,
He can never be mistook
More especially for a shamrock
Pinned atop 'is tricorn hat,
Over hair so long and straggly
Strugglin' from a week-old plait.

And 'is beard's aflamed and ginger
So much so it looks alight,
Burning like the witches cauldron
Fuelled with spells and burning bright,
And 'is eyes don't work together
When he's had a drink or two,
One looks off to right while t'other
Has a different point of view!

Some may think he be an eejit,
Others say he's full of guff
When 'is cup flows full of whisky
And he sneezes wi' the snuff
But I gotta make it clear now
Whether leprechaun or not,
When yer fluthered wi' a notion,
It be ludicrous, somewhat!

O'Leary

Now O'Leary is the keeper
of the gold at Rainbow's End,
bet yer never thought there was one -
but I'm telling yer my friend,
he be there in spring and summer
when the days are warm and dry
and the flies are fast abuzzin' ....
(so annoyingly not shy!)

In the autumn when 'tis blowin'
louder than a bellows roar
and the chestnut leaves are falling
fast across the woodland floor,
then O'Leary dons a waistcoat,
fleecy-lined to keep him snug -
as a dormouse hibernating
in a straw-filled garden trug.

And in winter when 'tis colder
than the river running deep,
when O'Leary's hands are frozen
and the birds no longer cheep,
then I tell yer 'tis a wonder
that O'Leary guards at all,
through the wind and hail and snowstorms,
sittin' by the waterfall.

'Tis the gold that McNamara
found in days of long- ago,
down a mine-shaft long forgotten
fer I'm sure you'd like to know.
Ever since ....
A rainbows glistened
shining every coloured hue,
that O'Leary takes good care of -
fer the likes of me and you!!!

The Shoemaker

O'Shea's made all the leprechauns'
their shoes for many years,
too many some might say for he
is older than he 'pears,
but lately's made a few mistakes
not many, only some -
yet 'nough to set the tongues awag
with due delirium.

'Twas only yesterday I hear
when stitching buttons to
the baker boy's tough working boot
that should o' been a shoe!
Then missed a cobblin' hammer-tap
so making fingers red
and swollen like pork sausages,
or so I hear it said.

Sometimes when memory deflates
he might forget to sew
a buckle, shiney bright and new,
or on a shoe a bow
but Cricket helps out where he can
and stays right by his side,
reminding him of orders due
from dawn to eventide.

There's times he works beyond the light
so candle wax is lit,
especially when in busy times
and all is off-target,
that's when he's ever vigilante
'cause recently he seared,
a slipper for the faerie queen
and set light to 'is beard!

O'Flannigan

O'Flannigan's a traveller,
He'll tell yer so 'imself,
With no abode to rest 'is feet
'pon stool or mantle-shelf,
He's wandered all 'is life, *he has,*
From Donegal to Cork
And even crossed the sea one time
With cousin Pat O'Rourke.

They sailed from Derry in the north
'cross to the Isle of Skye,
With each a knapsack full of ham,
Colcannon and a pie
And toadstools big as saucepan lids
To shelter from the rain
And ointment from the witch 'erself,
For Flannigan's chilblain.

They landed close to Staffin Bay
To ramble mile 'pon mile,
From north to south, then east to west
Across that Scottish isle,
At times they rode in pony-traps,
One day a caravan
With scenes painted in every hue,
As only tinkers' can.

Alas, they didn't stay for long,
O'Rourke missed 'is colleen,
O' Flannigan was homesick too
For Dublin's own cuisine -
Where soda bread at breakfast time
And gubeen served with tea,
Is all a leprechaun can wish
When clocks say five to three.

Of course yer'll think O'Flannigan
Has nowhere he calls home,
But home is where 'is hat maybe,
Where'er he likes to roam.
'afore the day turns into night
He'll stretch and with a yawn,
Lay down 'is weary head on moss
'til day follers the dawn.

Abigail

I can't remember, can't recall the day I heard the tale
of Michael J O'Lafferty's young sow called Abigail,
who on a wet and wint'ry night an' soaked beyond her skin,
fer sure decided time was right to find her next of kin.

An' so it was she bid farewell right there and then fer sure,
without a backward glance at all she set off 'cross the moor,
with ne'er a thought of where to go whilst stumblin' here and there,
disturbin' no-one 'cept herself, some rabbits and a hare !

She didn't know quite where it was her next of kin could be -
an' knew not where without a doubt of their locality,
an' now the rain had turned to sleet with cold she'd never known,
an' suddenly her old pig-sty was calling her back home.

From black as night she hurried home, to light of early dawn -
before her oinks be missed at all, or grunts dismissed with scorn,
an' thought perhaps things weren't that bad here in the light of day,
where ev'rything she'd ever known was here in Galway Bay.

An' so it is you'll catch a glimpse, (If lucky you should be)
of Michael J O'Lafferty slow winding o'er the lea -
with piglets borne by Abigail, who yearned fer next of kin
an' so was blessed with three in all, named Dolly, Rose and Flynn !

Devlin

His hat is taller than 'imself,
with cat-bells round the brim
and patches here and there-withal,
mis-matching faded trim.
He's small as only leprechauns
can be at Rainbow's End,
where fairy-folk and forest elves
with pixies oft' descend.

He'll not divulge his age to you,
a secret *to be sure,*
But in the glade where gossip's rife
'tis said, he's ninety four!
A lean, be-whiskered scoundrel now
but kindly none the less,
and should you meet with him you'll see
no hint of awfullness.

His baccy pipe is ancient now,
a comfort, *sure enough,*
Along with clover in his tea
and cherry flavoured snuff.
Some say he's quite forgetful though
while others never care -
if Devlin goes a day or two
not knowing who nor where.

He's wizened, *to be sure, he is*
and spinning's *still* his trade,
with finest wool he'll spin for you
a cloth with matching braid.
Sometimes he'll spin the whole day through,
more oft' though *not at all,*
'twill all depend if Connelly,
his friend pays him a call.

They sit for hours with idle craic
cross-legged upon the ground
and blarney Coleens passing by,
no matter lean or round,
until that is, their cups are dry
with limericks well-versed,
then naught is left *at all, at all* -
to quench their 'normous thirst

'Tis only when old Connelly
heads off down the boreen,
that Devlin turns for home at last
with thoughts for his drisheen,
then later when he feels the urge,
p'haps he'll spin some more -
until that is, old Connelly
knocks once again his door.

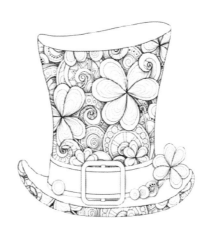

The Leprechaun's Craic

'Tis often said that leprechauns can spin a yarn or two,
Especially when their cups are full of Auntie Meg's home-brew,
Fer only then the stories told can last a day or more,
Until that is the fiddler plays an' all join the furore.
With toothless grins to spin the craic they'll take turns with a jig,
Their shoe-buckles fast clatterin' that cease only to swig
The potent brew from elderflower made many months afore,
Fermented with a secret spell behind a secret door.

Fineen is usually the first an' Quinn brings up the rear,
While Clooney's never far behind to spread the atmosphere,
With poteens of the finest grog an' limericks galore,
'Tis everyone and everyone ends gigglin' on the floor.
When laughter rings across the Dell an' hats are all askew,
'Tis as it is, I tell you now, 'til Auntie Meg's home-brew
Has all been drunk with ev'ry drop licked from the poteen jars,
An' each an' ev'ry leprechaun's asleep beneath the stars.

Macanally's Band

There was a night so long ago when sleep was far away,
At five years old I tossed and fought with pillow and duvet.
Thus, from my rumpled bed I crept to find my Granpa's gift,
A fife made from the finest wood found on the Shannon's drift.
He said it was a magic fife with charms to call upon,
Whereby the leprechauns will come, but warned they'd, '*carry on.*'
With eyes tight shut I pursed my lips to play the secret chord
And suddenly the door flung wide to leave me over-awed.

In stripey socks and velvet suits, with fingers long and slim,
They played banjos and wooden flutes in shoes with buckled trim.
With introductions all around I shook hands with them all -
Old Macannally's Band it was, direct from Donegal.
Old Fergus had the longest beard and with his cousin Hugh
Played tabor pipes and tambourine with hats that sat askew!
A horn-pipe then a single jig were danced by Master Quinn,
Who tickled both my hands and toes and begged me, 'come join in.'

A concertina played by Sean and fiddle by Fineen,
Was just about the very best a girl of five had seen
And Sweeney with his pointy ears was magic on the spoons,
With every triple 'click-it-y, a bonus to the tunes.
Some came to sing and some to dance a jig to tap your feet,
With reels and drumbeats to entrance to mark time with each beat
And as they whirled around my room, bewhiskered, small yet wise,
Old Macannally cried, '*hoorah'* and rapped his bony thighs.

They sang of stardust sprinkle-ings to make the shamrocks grow,
Where everything was painted green (f*or they'd have you to know*).
While Daley sang of 'Father Flynn' and 'Roses of Tralee,'
Before an Irish lullaby was sung by Quinn for me.
Please let me be just five again to see those leprechauns,
With mischief, dance around my feet before the morning dawns,
And let the laughter ring out loud from Irish eyes that shine,
Just as 'twas said so long ago, the stars shone out of mine!

Wash Day

'Tis six in the mornin'
As Monday is dawnin'
In far away Dinkelly Dell,
The laundry is waitin',
There's no hesitatin'
As water's brought up from the well.
With vigour there's scrubbin',
Some dabbin' and rubbin'
A stain on a night-shirt lapel,
With plenty of bashin',
'Pon washboards a thrashin'
As soap bubbles up in a swell.

'Tis all of a hurry -
For Missus MacMurray,
Her drawers, she needs quick as a wink
And don't leave 'em powd'ry,
'Tween lace and embroid'ry
And don't let the whites run with pink.
Her cousin's to marry
So no time to tarry,
She needs 'em 'afore you can blink,
While stockings fer Paddy,
Wee Finnegan's laddie
Are wool and so likely to shrink!

'Tis young Lucy Rainbow
Who without a shadow,
Will bustle 'bout more on wash-day,
In apron and bandeau,
Her voice a crescendo
She rinses stains clean all-away.
Especially tomato
And fruits from the hedgerow
Made into a berry sundae,

While out in the meadow
The sheets start to billow,
With smells of a summer bouquet.

Flannery's Dilemma

'Twas Halloween and all not well
in Flannery's small garden,
where year on year his squashes grow,
with peat to make them harden,
but this year one was oversize
and Flannery, who's none too wise
was pond'rin how to gather in
his harvest of a prized pumpkin.

He heaved with spade trying to haul,
with all his strength he mustered,
alas, the shovel broke in two
and Flannery grew flustered,
but late that night while over-wrought,
he had another gin and thought,
if only he could find haulage,
his troubles would be but a smidge.

Next day while musing on his plight
to move the pumpkin hither,
he saw before his gin-filled eyes
two mice, Dawdle and Dither,
so with a harness round each girth,
they pulled together with great mirth,
the pumpkin that would make the pie -
on Halloween when witches fly.

Paddy O'Mara

If you hap' to have a button
That may need a little thread,
'Pon a coat that needs repairing
But with still some wear ahead,
Or yer dress may need a ribbon
For to bring it up to date,
To the fashion of the moment
Which yer love to emulate.

I suggest yer see O'Mara,
He's a tailor and I hear
He can work a dozen wonders
Making garments less austere,
With a dart betwixt yer shoulders
Or a pleat about mid-waist,
He'll transform yer older garments
With dexterity and grace.

He may charge a golden sovereign,
Or a penny, it depends
On the time he takes re-modelin'
Any up and comin' trends,
But be sure what e'er the weather,
Be it shine or rain or hail,
He can have yer garments ready
'Fore you've read a fairytale.

Course yer'll have a job to find him
For his name ain't in the book,
He's a leprechaun I tells yer
And he lives in County Cooke,
Where the best-dressed folk are dwellin'
And 'tis good to be alive -
Should yer hap' to find O'Mara,
'Twixt the hours of nine to five.

Creatures Great and Small

Dandy Toad

Should you come into my garden
On a sunny afternoon,
When my rose blooms with abandon
In the merry month of June,
You'll see Dandy Toad paradin'
Round and round the lily pond,
Never cross or mis-behavin'
Never venturing beyond.
In his coat of purple velvet
O'er his shirt of finest lace,
With a kerchief in his pocket
He's the epitome of grace,
Culminating in such grandeur
As I've never seen before,
From a relative or lodger
Mister or a Monsignor.
His display of masqueradin'
Is the funniest of sights,
A charade of mimic takin'
In his spats and stripey tights,
And his top-hat with a feather
(Which he stole from Gandy Goose,)
Gives him carte blanche any weather –
To recite from Dr Seuss.
So be warned if you should visit,
Dandy likes to steal the show
But I'll serve you tea and biscuit
And record a video ......

Hope

At five past the midnight
When I rose from sleep,
The dawning of Christmas
Was snow ankle deep,
On hearing commotions
I crept down the stairs,
Expecting a burglar
To catch unawares.

Intently, I listened,
Oh my! What a shock,
I saw Father Christmas
Was picking our lock!
'I'm no thief, he sighed,
'Please don't be afraid
I bring Christmas tidings,
With postage prepaid.'

His coat of soft velvet
Was ancient and red,
And snowy white poms-poms
He wore on his head.
Then brought from his knapsack
For under the tree,
A doll for my daughter
And perfume for me.

Twas then, I saw wriggle
From under his hat
The sweetest, dear puppy
That fell to the mat.
We both stood there laughing
As puppy ran free,
To play with a bauble
Hung low on the tree.

And there in the lamplight
He held out his hand,
To whisper a secret
Not long ago planned.
'This puppy is special
To watch over you,
With friendship and comfort
You'll rarely feel blue.'

With a tear in my eye
And a wag from his tail,
I cradled the puppy
So small and so pale.
'Your daughter lies poorly,'
I heard Santa say,
'And your husband's at war -
So can't get away.'

'He wrote, you were lonely
And would I call in -
'Cos maybe, sometime 'fore
He sees all his kin.
He thought a cute puppy
Might help ease your pain,
Until he can hold you
Close to him again.'

'The puppy will help you
Through hard times ahead,
For Hope is her namesake
So keep her well-fed.
Come, dry all your tears now
You've plenty to do,
Hope needs a cool drink
and something to chew.'

'Twas then we heard calling
From Rudolph outside,

For Santa to hurry
And quicken his stride,
He shook all the sleigh bells
Whilst I dried a tear,
As Santa was whisprin' ....
'I'll see you next year!!!'

Majella Magpie

She's friend to all the faerie-folk,
especially the Queen,
who tends to seek Majella's help
when troubles intervene,
or when she needs a recipe
to tempt the faerie King
with pies and tarts and sticky fudge,
in fact most anything.

Her kitchen in the maple tree's
beyond the orchard where,
she gathers fruit for all her pies
in bowls of earthenware -
while in the larder neatly piled
are berries tucked away,
to fill Majella's pastry case
made only yesterday.

Majella's fondant cakes are best,
as all the faeries know,
with icing pink as candyfloss
or paler than the snow,
yet dear Majella has been known
to sprinkle faerie dust
'pon one or two deliveries,
When naughtiness seems just!

She'll need a mental push at times
When souffles fail to rise,
Or when her sugar burns like toast
Before her very eyes,
But long before the silv'ry moon
Knocks gently on her door,
Majella's baked an extra tray
Of faerie cakes, threescore.

Mariella Mongoose

Now Mariella I've been told
is neither young nor very old,
brown-eyed, petite with pointed chin,
and fur mid-grey, o'er pinkish skin,
but 'cording to the nearby trees
her temper'd make your marrow freeze.

She snaps at this and then at that
if someone's near her habitat,
concealed below the termite hill
now sadly, empty, quietly still –
since Mariella without care
moved in, presenting them a scare!

With paws outstretched, her mouth agape
she'll chase away most any shape,
and who is it to wonder why
should any cobra coil nearby,
or scorpion with poisoned tail
be long harassed to no avail.

Alas, a lonely smile she had
one day when she was mostly mad,
sat curled beneath the cedar's bough
less holier with raised eyebrow,
'perhaps I'll be more kind', she said,
'and not be such a noodle-head.'

The trees all smiled; they understood
she wasn't bad but far from good,
the cedar thought it rather strange
but offered help to make her change -
with great diplomacy and tact,
such qualities she wholly lacked.

I heard it said she changed in days
her thund'rous ill bad tempered ways,
no longer smug but happy now -
sat curled beneath the cedar's bough,
her friend ....the greatest tree of all,
beneath the sun in Senegal.

The Fox

He stalks in silence dark as night,
Beneath the moonlit breathless skies,
When feathers, black are in full flight,
And all around are fearful cries
Through swathes of swirling mist tonight,
He's guided by the fireflies.

He lies in wait by the lagoon,
His shadow in a pool of ink,
As crickets chant their sombre tune,
And in the distance eyes that blink
Are warmly golden like the moon,
Yet peer at him without a wink.

A game, he plays of hide and seek,
And suddenly with fearless heart,
He zig zags in a burnished streak,
To snare his quarry, not so smart,
Who was unwise to pip a squeak,
And make a feast of al a carte.

He can't dispute that life is sweet,
When all the craft and guile he's used,
Gave splendours that he's had to eat,
Without becoming harmed or bruised
So with his appetite replete,
He sleeps in silence .... quite bemused.

The Tired Bear (Quartern)

When honey bees tickle my nose
Just as I lay my head to dream,
Of salmon I hope to expose
Beneath the mountain in midstream.

My soft brown eyes open with rage
When honeybees tickle my nose,
For I'm a bear of tender age
And in the sun I like to doze.

I growl a snore with soft bellows
But cannot close my tired eyes,
When honeybees tickle my nose
And buzz like demons in the skies.,

When finally I rest my head
I dream of honey, I suppose,
Instead of salmon over-fed
When honeybees tickle my nose.

Bear with A Sore Head

I once knew a brown bear called Sally
Who with a wasp became pally
But the wasp stung her nose
And you rightly suppose
That Sally has gone quite doolally!!!

The Unicorn

Here in the forest in dawn's early rain
I sigh, for I know what I'll see,
Hoping by magic to catch sight again,
Of the unicorn, wand'ring free.
Her mane ruffles on the cold silent breeze,
In skies that are broody and deep,
While herons fly, calling to whisprin' trees,
Awakening meadows from sleep.

She dwells in a land where dragons reside,
Where witches can cast you a spell
And goblins will curse and even provide
For wizards, some toads and cadelle.
Mention the unicorn, tales will unfold
Of spirits that come back to life,
To roam evermore with blood that is cold,
Thus causing encounters with strife.

Gold is her horn and 'tis sparkling with sheen
And she's paler than rippling sand,
All beauty is here that you've never seen,
For this is a magical land.
With nostrils aflare she looks to the sky
Whilst drinking the dew from the mist,
Then turning around she looks in my eye -
With magic, I'm instantly kissed.

I stand here and watch without any fear,
As stars and the moon rendezvous,
For I never thought I'd ever get near
This legend so many pursue.
Her tail is now swishing with a new scent
And her ears are pricked for a chirr,
As I must depart with tears of content,
To treasure my memories of her.

Miss Sissy Stork

Miss Sissy Stork was getting on
And every year or thereupon,
Her memory would have a lapse,
Was it old age? Well, yes perhaps.
When young she flew both far and wide
Taking her orders from each bride,
With pen and pad she wrote it down,
A boy or girl and in which town
And sometimes quads and sometimes quins,
Or by demand just one or twins
And should the eyes be brown or blue,
With paler skin or darker hue.
By memory she got it right,
Delivering when dark or light
To house or flat or bungalow,
Miss Sissy Stork would always know.

But lately something's wholly lacked
For Sissy lost her way, in fact
Not once or twice but more I've heard,
She's fast become a wayward bird!
Each cloud now looks just like the rest
From Benidorm to Bucharest,
Through Canada and far Bombay
And all along the Milky Way,
The angels keep a watch on her
As Sissy's eyesight's now a blur
And so the angels bought a map
To help dear Sissy to recap,
Just where her babies need to be,
Which town, indeed which addressee,
For babies need to be on time,
Without mishaps or pantomime,

So, Sissy with spectacles on
And map to hand can liaison,
Still taking orders from each bride
From everywhere, both far and wide.
When Cupid takes a well earned rest
Sissy will do her very best
To babysit, just for a while
And though no longer as agile,
She'll walk the babies through the park
Where birds will sing and dogs will bark
And trees will sway and stoop and bow,
When seeing Sissy Stork, they'll sough,
Simply because they hold respect
For Sissy, who with intellect
Will bring your baby, no delay,
Nine months from order, come what may!!

Kitten Trixiebelle

As Trixiebelle sat by the pond
One cool September night,
A moonbeam fell from who knows where
To cast a dazzling light.
Now Trixiebelle was very young,
So rooted to the spot
When from nowhere a pixie flew,
Perfumed with bergamot.

Beyond the breeze she heard whispers
Of lilting lullabies
And suddenly from everywhere
In view before her eyes,
Were fairy folk in silver gowns
With ribbons trailing far,
Floating around on gauzy wings,
Flaunting their repertoire.

Upon the willow's cool green leaves
The ladybirds looked on,
As were the beetles smiling broad
And from the reeds a swan.
While sitting on a birch catkin
A fairy waved her wand
And hurriedly from who knows where,
All life astired the pond.

The moon was high and waiting there
For stars to take their place,
While on the pond, on lily pads
Toads laughing swam a race
And all the while young Trixiebelle
Blinked eyes as wide as sky,
As elves as small as her front paw,
On butterflies flew by.

And as the oak tree gently swayed
With long and graceful boughs,
A fairy with silvery hair
Tickled her soft eyebrows
And as a breeze blew from nowhere
Relieving Summer's heat,
Around the garden and the pond,
All was alluring, sweet.

And then from goodness knows somewhere
She heard her mistress call,
With warnings she must go inside
To shelter from rainfall,
So with farewells on velvet paws
She left the magic scene,
To dream of heaven knows but what,
She'd seen upon the green!

Thimble

Now Thimble is I have been told
not very young nor very old,
you'll think me rash and quite absurd
but Thimble thinks she is a bird.
Each day she flies with pied wagtails
over the hills and through the vales,
while oak trees talk above her head,
'just give her time,' is all they've said.

The willow tits, sparrows and crow,
along with chaffinch seem to know
that Thimble thinks she is a bird
but no-one seems to say a word.
The eiders with their fluffy down
and sparrows with their feathers brown,
built her a nest of woven hair
as soft as cashmere, I declare!

Down where the river gently stirs
beneath the singing conifers,
'tis here the birds gather to rest
and Thimble comes at their request.
The goldfinch, dunnock and cuckoo
along with waxwings rendezvous,
when bats take flight to dart and skim
and sunlight starts to tremble dim.

There in the midst is Thimble, sweet
with little hands and little feet,
sitting upon soft scented grass
as owls with moths go drifting past.
Her fairy wings she tightly furls,
as fast asleep she gently curls
and in the quiet and the hush,
sweet lullabies are sung by thrush.

A Kitten's Tale

She purred beneath the fairy dust,
Her whiskers twitching to and fro
As there upon the lawn she sat
Just by the patch of sweet marrow.
She'd curled within her basket warm
Hoping she would soon find her sleep,
But whispers pricked her tufted ears
And so she thought she'd take a peep.

The stars were twinkling overhead
And shone upon her tabby fur,
But just beyond the gravel path
Saw movement by the blue larkspur.
Like most cats she was curious
So crept with back low to the ground,
Towards the little patch of light
That glowed above the fairy mound.

Beguiled by this magical sight
Of fairies with sweet lilting cries
And pixie folk riding slow snails,
With cheers to greet and socialise
And in cool puddles left by rain,
Some fairies dipped their little toes
Then laughed when hearing her meow,
While pixies tickled her wet nose.

Her fur is dusted with sequins
From fairies singing with delight
Just as the moon blows her a kiss,
Among the stars so pearly-white.
Now purring, stretching with a yawn,
Her whiskers twitching to and fro,
As out of sleep she slowly comes,
To ponder why her furs aglow!

The Tiger and The Silver Moon

The moon shines brightest when the stars are twinkling,
Counting the hours through the darkest night,
Below the blue lagoon and purple mountains
Is where the tiger stays until daylight.

There is no breeze astir amongst the bull reeds,
Like soldiers standing round the blue lagoon
And here will lay the tiger till the morning,
Just dreaming by the glare of the full moon.

Beneath the moon she's neither cold nor lonely,
For laying by her side there is a king,
The lion is the king of all surrounds them
And far beyond where darkened shadows cling.

The tiger as a kitten was abandoned,
Within a few still hours of her birth
And left to wander mountains cold and silent
Where terrors of the jungle rule the earth.

But as the baby tiger lay there starving,
Without a voice save for a whimp'ring cry,
The moon dipped low and casting not a shadow
Just swept her up onto a cloud nearby.

The far sky came to smile upon the baby,
Now laying in the wisps of gauzy cloud
And told the moon about a lonely lion,
By a lagoon and roaring ever loud.

And so the moon decided in his wisdom
That lion and the tiger rendezvous,
The far sky smiled and said ever so kindly,
Arrangements would be made without to do.

But something happened to the baby tiger,
It seemed her coat of red had become white,
For when the moon had found her on the mountain
The glow of silver sprinkled her with light.

The moon shines brightest when the stars are twinkling
And all is still around the blue lagoon,
As side by side the lion and white tiger,
Sit 'neath the silver glare of the full moon.

Ezmerelda

Way on down the Mississippi where the river slowly bends,
Lives a 'gator Ezmerelda known as Ezzy to her friends.
She's a wise old alligator with a twinkle in her eye,
More espec'lly when young curlews bake her fav'rite pecan pie.

When the sun's high in the morning in the mangrove swamp she'll
lay,
With perhaps a catfish smiling watching pelicans at play,
Or the gophers busy chasing anything that will allow
Near the roots of the old maple, 'neath the over-hanging bough.

After mid-day when it's hotter than a furnace burning bright,
Ezzy wallows 'til it's cooler as the sun dips out of sight,
Where the cormorants are restin' with the pretty whitetail deer,
And the cranes stoop ever silent where the water's cool and clear.

Ezzy likes a bedtime story while beneath the tulip tree,
When the skeeters cease abuzzin' their incessant comment'ry,
Way on down the Mississippi where the river slowly bends,
You'll find Ezmerelda 'gator reading to her 'ssippi friends.

Pumpkin

My cat with fur as dark as ink
Lies patient for her prey,
Unseen amid the orchard trees
Where fallen apples lay.
On velvet paws and with pretence
She peers with eyes agape,
Below the glow from sequined stars
As shadows softly drape.

I hear perhaps a thousand tongues
In chorus on the fringe,
Where Pumpkin, with her saffron eyes
Awaits her next challenge.
She's stalking where she can't be seen,
Alone and crouched, until
Bewitched by moonshine all around
She waits her chance to kill.

I cannot hear a single purr -
Or see a whisker tweak,
But suddenly in her front paws
I hear a morsel squeak.
Her hunting skills are next to none,
Of this I can't deny,
With pride she'll bring her quarry home,
When dawn alights the sky.

Give Me The Moon ....

The Moon and The Morning

The moon's slow disappearing to the far side of the sky
To shine with stars on lovers far away,
But here you hold me closer on a whisper with a sigh
As shadows turn from violet to grey.

Below the rising of the dawn there's voice nor foot astir,
So warm from sleep I take your hand in mine,
And on a murmur softer than a kitten's gentle purr
I taste love sweeter than a southern wine.

And where a chorus rises from below where crickets hide,
Beneath where willows weep all in a row,
There's neither peace nor silence for the lonely moon to ride
Above the heavens, drifting to and fro.

I see as morning circles over trees of green and gold
Around the stars pale in the borrowed light,
Their sequins kissing pearl-white mist as morning hours unfold,
Then with the moon slip gently out of sight.

High up and round and shining o'er the land for you and I,
The moon embraces morning in the stainless blue of sky.

The Moonbeam

I found a moonbeam long ago to hold within my hand,
Enchantment only few could know transported to a land,
Where all the earth is marzipan and treacle are the seas
Beneath the moon, a gentleman, made wholly out of cheese.

He shines by day instead of night, confusing witchy crones,
On sticks of broom as fast as light above the vast unknowns,
O'er valleys made of birthday cake and trees of choc'late whirls,
While faeries busy custom-make meringues with toffee swirls.

There's candyfloss and strawb'ry ice, or anything you wish,
Served only if you're smile is nice on plate or fancy dish,
While mice are sugar-pink and small and gingerbread are men,
Made extra broad and extra tall from five inch up to ten!

The land is every coloured hue, with peppermint green sky,
As kangaroos play peek-a-boo in lemon grass knee-high,
While unicorns in chequered pants play jousting, unaware
Of weasels chasing spotty ants, away to who knows where.

Along the river rainbow carp sing awf'ly out of tune,
While otters try to sing B sharp with hopes the catfish swoon,
And ladybirds in fancy dress enjoy the jamboree,
With Lion and his Lioness in total harmony.

I found a moonbeam long ago that led me to a world,
Where faerie-tales own sweet tableau's forever oyster-pearled.

Moon-maids

When the moon's slow chasing shadows with a mystifying smile,
Each step upon the snow's a pool of ink,
But when I'm still and very still and standing like a stone
I watch it slowly shrivel, spill and shrink.

There's neither wind nor breath astir as stars gently bestrewn
The moon now dancing for my own delight,
And magic are the voices coming from the forest floor
As moon maids gather, silver-sheened and white.

I sit as quiet as any mouse to watch them at their play,
Beneath the moon and mountainside so tall,
But soon the maids forget me there and think they are alone
To dance around my feet where shadows fall.

They have small need of any sleep until the dawn peeps through,
When petal-cups awake, their blooms unfurled,
Meanwhile the moon maids here and now I'll watch over again,
Up from beneath the magic of the world.

Shadows

When the moon is full of laughter
With sunlight castaway,
Ever glowing and majestic -
In skies of charcoal grey.
There are shadows softly creeping
Within my garden wall,
Ever strange and mystifying,
While leaves of autumn fall.

They scamper 'tween the orchards
And tease with peek-a-boo
My hedgehog peering out beneath
The rickety lean-to –
Some beg a game of hide-and-seek
From spider, black as night,
Appraising morsels for his tea,
Ignoring shadow's plight!

Shy tabby cat won't play their games,
She'll glance the other way,
With ne'er a care for anything,
Specially shadow's play –
And when I'm quickly running home,
They scare the life from me -
When the moon's still full of laughter,
The shadows stalk with glee!

Rebel Moon

I found love 'neath a rebel moon,
There where the path spreads north,
Where mermaids disappear too soon -
As seas toss back and forth.

'Cross the land to the savage sea,
Beyond the ancient path,
My lover pledged his heart to me,
With neither rage nor wrath.

No longer do the willows weep,
Above where otters dive,
In streams and rivers not too deep,
Where I no longer strive.

Below the rebel moon and stars,
The good Lord set me free -
To see beyond Pluto and Mars
And all the world to see.

I linger here within my home -
Safe from the rebel moon,
Where seas tossing with spewing foam,
No longer call the tune!

The Moon's Own Land (Kyrielle)

The crescent of the moon drifts high
Across the darkest, velvet sky,
Where I shall hold her silver hand,
Then travel to the moon's own land.

She'll scoop me up and on a sigh,
We'll sail through stars to Gemini,
Or stroll on Neptune's rippling sand,
Then travel to the moon's own land.

Pluto will wave and Mars will call,
For he's the solar know it all,
I'll marvel as I understand,
Then travel to the moon's own land.

I'll serenade you with delight
And kiss the beauty of the night,
Deep scented with each starry strand,
Then travel to the moon's own land.

And as I'm shimmering aloft,
Sprinkled with sequins glit'ring soft,
I'll witness shooting stars disband,
Then travel to the moon's own land.

O'er silken skies where stars lie deep,
And o'er the land where you're asleep,
Your dreams I'll scatter as I planned,
Then travel to the moon's own land.

Moonshine Cats

When half the world lies deep in sleep
And winter nights are cold with chill,
With only shadows left to peep
Around the garden, tired and still.
The gold of autumn's clearly gone,
No longer do my roses smile,
Yet violets still linger on
Beneath the gorse in single file.

The only smile I see tonight
Glows from the bubble of the moon,
As cats on rooftops bathe in light
With talk of going mousing soon.
Some cats are fat and some are thin
And some quite mad with silly names,
While some create an awful din
Should they be playing mating games.

They care not that I have to rest
Below their yawning caterwaul,
For in the night they seem obsessed,
No matter if they're big or small.
By day they're all somewhat aloof,
But night for me comes all too soon,
For then they gather on my roof
To dance a jig beneath the moon.

Now certain of their mystic powers
From midnight 'til the light of dawn,
No matter if it's dry or showers,
In hurricanes, or windswept torn.
For there is nothing enjoyed more,
As I account for countless sheep -
And they escape the cat-flap door,
When half the world lies deep in sleep.

In Remembrance ....

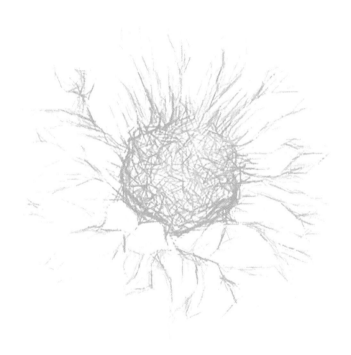

The 11th Hour

Today we're at the cenotaph
With poppy wreaths to lay,
Beneath a sky with threats of rain
On this Armistice Day.

It seems forever we have prayed
For those sent off to wars,
To fight for freedom for this land
Then die on foreign shores.

Some lie upon a windswept hill,
Yet many in a grave
Still side by side in comradeship,
All heroes and *all* brave.

Warm tears they'll never see from kin,
Nor taste love from a kiss,
Nor hear a baby's urgent cry,
Nor walk softly in mist.

My prayers are with the countless names
That march in unity,
Held in the winds own cool embrace
For all eternity.

In silence and all shining plain
Beneath the flags that fly,
Where all around are faces that
Must surely feel as I!

Today we're at the cenotaph
With poppy wreaths to lay,
Beneath a sky with threats of rain,
On this Armistice Day.

Marching Feet

'Tis at the cenotaph we stand this cool November day,
amid a sea of misery 'neath clouds of autumn grey.
Our mood is darkly sombre with emotions riding high,
while veterans salute the brave they'd hope would never die.

Like bloody corpses, poppies strewn, the cold grey cenotaph,
and I no longer read for tears the written epitaph.
The marching feet draw closer as I hear the women weep,
for those who died in battle, now eternally asleep.

How many kisses never kissed nor smiles no longer smiled,
now lay beneath conflicting lands so brutally defiled.
How many promises not kept nor letters not received,
how many saddened spouses are foresakenly aggrieved?

The Royal Marines take the salute to lead the marching feet,
while veterans, from many wars march to, 'Beating Retreat,'
their caps and medals proudly worn, boots *still* enhanced with shine,
who've fought conflicts across the globe now march in perfect time.

Now I am weeping openly to see such sacrifice,
to think these men laid down their lives for us and at what price,
so that our children's children can live a life that's free
and never know oppression from a war *they'd h*ave to flee.

The only sounds I hear today are those of marching feet,
of men and women crying at the melancholy beat,
for all those that are falling *still* that we may live in peace,
oh! Please God when will it stop, when will the fighting cease?

Too Soon Too Late

Too soon my friend to say goodbye
Too soon to grieve, too soon to cry
Too soon to miss you by my side
Too soon for tears I fail to hide

Too late to walk that extra mile -
Through fields of corn o'er yonder stile
On days when all the world is fine
With ne'er a thought for, 'auld lang syne'

Too soon to bid our sad farewell
Too soon to put me through this hell
Too soon for tears I'll sadly weep
Before we lay you down to sleep

Lament for a Red Beret

Go forward brave Paras, step into the breach,
All ranks of young men going out of our reach,
Our tears and embraces must now see you through,
For God knows how long, oh if we only knew.

Go follow your orders, you've sung lullabies
To babes in your arms with a tear in your eyes,
Your spirits will help you to campaign with pride,
Returning heroic, our prayers justified.

Go with our love lads, we wish you all well
As you take command in Afghanistan's hell.
You'll go on patrols into hostile terrain
Where the Taliban threat is so bloody insane!

Go into the wilderness of that far land,
When you come home lads you'll have a riband,
Another new medal, a further war fought,
Another stop press on a newsreel report.

Go valiant Paras beyond the hot sun
Where food is deprived and you sleep with your gun,
Trek over the hill lads and that far ravine
But watch where you tread lads, for mines are unseen.

Go pursue terrorists and the ringleader,
As you sought Hitler ..... go seek Al Queda,
Advance into battle with God by your side
And angels above you to guard and to guide.

Go onward brave Paras to seek out the scourge
Of raging insurgents, we'll sing you a dirge.
Your Red Berets wear with the highest esteem,
Maintaining your goals as you scream and blaspheme.

Go seek out your chaplain, kneel with him in prayer
and try making sense of this bloody warfare!
'Beat the Retreat' Paras, 'nough has been said,
Another Red Beret's among our war dead.
Amen

The Garden Party
For The Not Forgotten

We stroll away from work and strife
On lawns behind a wall,
Where sunlight pours like liquid gold
'Pon shadows where they fall.
Beneath a sky where fragrances,
From blooms whisper and stir,
Around the trees called London Planes
With boughs of royal grandeur.

Where medals worn with dignity
Cast shadows in the sun,
For comrades from the present day,
To those of World War One.
Their lives from one to millions,
Young or with wrinkles deep
Are honoured with the Royalty here,
As we try not to weep.

There's tinkling of bone china cups,
But voices in my ear,
Remind me of where corpses lay
As distant bells toll clear,
But life is spared to many more
And help we can't deny,
Lest we forget, why these men fought,
It was for you and I ....

'Buckingham Palace
Garden Party for The Not Forgotten'

I'll Bathe the Twins

I'll bathe the twins tonight mamma,
I'll sing a nursery rhyme,
I'll read them fairytales I heard
From you in my springtime.

I'll tell how crickets try to sing
In harmony all day.
To see the laughter in their eyes
At silly things I say.

I'll tell them how the fairy folk
On wings of fine white lace,
Shall take their baby teeth away
So new ones take their place.

I'll tell them of the seven seas,
That one day they may sail
And of the mermaids swimming there
Beyond the beach so pale.

I'll tickle each of all their toes
Just as you did to me,
Then kiss with cuddles when they laugh
And say, 'it's just a flea!'

I'll tell them how you used to bathe
Me when I was a child,
With soap as pink as candyfloss,
So gentle and so mild.

I'll tell them of the love I had
From you my dear mamma,
And how within the midnight sky
You are the brightest star.

Margot

Her tiny feet bled with the pain
From her last matinee,
A repertoire she knew so well,
She danced it every day.
En pointe her feet would pirouette,
Solo or pas de deaux,
In arabesque she looked divine
For I'm a connoisseur.

The spotlights loved her charisma,
And her extending arms
Flowed like a willow in the breeze,
Displaying all her charms.
Her glissades (gleesahds) made me skip a breath,
In floating pink chiffon
And in Giselle she stopped my heart,
As did her dying swan.

Her feet told many stories but
With each ballet performed,
She needed drugs to free the pain
Of toes that were deformed.
With Nureyev she found new life
That lasted many years,
He said, their bodies danced as one,
Their souls crossing frontiers.

With each chasse across the stage
And jete (shuh-tay) that she flew,
Margot Fonteyn was magical
En pointe in lace tutu.
Her tiny feet bled with the pain
From her last matinee,
A repertoire she knew so well,
Until her dying day.

Dolly Daydream

My Dolly with her brown eyes sweet
and dainty ballerina feet,
affectionate, with heart of gold,
I'm sure God surely lost the mould.

I found her on a rainy day,
as cars drove fast sending their spray,
onto this little dog so lost
and freezing in the morning's frost.

Her coat was sorely massed with fleas,
as I bent low upon my knees,
to scoop her safe within my arms,
enraptured by her canine charms.

My house she found so warm she stayed
and over years she's never strayed,
instead she's become my best friend,
assured with me she can depend.

It was a cold, wet day in spring,
this little dog pulled my heart string.
When I was low she brought me love,
sent by an angel from above.

The first time she sat on my knee
I felt the need for poetry,
so with a pen I wrote a line
and suddenly the world was mine.

Dolly

Catherine

He said there never was a rose more lovelier than her
Nor yet a poet to compose a song if you prefer,
To croon as moon and stars enclose while foxes gently stir,
Then hunt where no man ever goes for mice with velvet fur.

He said she was his golden fall, his summer and his spring,
His tower of strength, his rock, his wall, his life, his everything,
In skies of grey 'neath winter's pall when blooms cease flowering,
As we succumb to winter's call; she made him feel a king.

He said her smile could light the skies forever and a day,
Sometimes with mirth but ever wise to light the Milky Way,
As twilight shone within her eyes when clouds were pink and grey,
And afternoon had said goodbyes, as people sometimes say.

He never thought he'd be alone before the winter's snow,
Before the willows could atone for weeping ever low,
Beyond the lake where she was known and where now in a row,
Around her beautiful headstone a rose shall always grow.

The Last Post

Come blow your bugle soldier boy,
Come blow your bugle loud,
That we may this Remembrance Day
Stand firm and ever proud.
Come blow your bugle mournfully,
For heroes, everyone -
Are they who perished before time
In conflicts lost and won.
Come blow your bugle softly now
For us to mourn the dead,
Who gave their lives in Flanders Fields -
With blood unduly shed
And on a melancholy note,
We'll think of those near home,
In World War II and battles since
Where'er the war lords roam!
Come blow your bugle soldier boy,
Come blow a thousandfold,
Lest we forget within our time -
For they shall not grow old!

Come blow your bugle soldier boy,
Come blow your bugle loud!

Biography

Lulu Gee lives on the North Kent coast of England with her husband Daniel Lake, the acclaimed war poet and who collaborated with Lulu on her two previous books. She has one daughter who makes the most amazing quilts and a grandson reading law at University.

Her love of fantasy and the natural world has long inspired Lulu, enabling her to write in any genre as the mood takes her and she has a fast growing following of her work from the many poetry recitals she gives to the younger generation.

She was delighted to be made an honorary director of The International Poetry Fellowship (IPF) in 2013 and the same year won the much coveted Vera Rich memorial prize for her acclaimed poem, 'Cumbria.' In 2014 she won The Elizabeth Barrett Browning memorial prize for, 'The Bride' and in 2015 was awarded Poet Laureate by Prism Anthology. Her poem, 'The Bride' also received acclaim on Radio Jersey (USA), October 2018.

Lulu has been published in well over 150 anthologies worldwide and hopes to still be writing for many more years to come.

Picture Index

34611018R00144

Printed in Poland
by Amazon Fulfillment
Poland Sp. z o.o., Wrocław